Colin Spencer is a novelist, playwright, artist and jour-
nalist who has also written for film and televison.

Since giving up eating meat, he has written several
cookery books, most recently *Cordon Vert* published by
Thorsons. He has had nine novels published which have
earned him much praise and a wide following. He is also
well known as a playwright both in Britain and on the
Continent. *Spitting Image* was staged in London's West
End, and *The Sphinx Mother* was given its world prem-
ière at the Salzburg Festival in 1972.

He has lived and travelled extensively in Europe, and
now writes a regular food column for the *Guardian*.

He has always had an enthusiasm for fish and the
various methods of cooking it, some of which he learnt
on his travels.

Colin Spencer's

FISH
COOKBOOK

BRACKEN

This 1994 edition distributed by Bracken Books,
an imprint of Studio Editions Ltd.,
Princess House, 50 Eastcastle Street,
London W1N 7AP, England.

First published in 1986 by Pan Books Ltd.

Text and illustrations copyright © Colin Spencer 1986
Photographs copyright © Roger Phillips 1986

ISBN 1-85891-213-X

Printed in Great Britain by Mackays

CONTENTS

INTRODUCTION

Fish in the unruffled lakes
Their swarming colours wear,
Swans in the winter air
A white perfection have,
And the great lion walks
Through his innocent grove;
Lion, fish, and swan
Act, and are gone
Upon Time's toppling wave.

W. H. Auden,
'*Fish in the unruffled lakes*'
(1936)

In Britain, we live on islands surrounded by a vast diversity of fish. There are 370 species of fish in our seas, rivers and lakes. Yet for centuries we have been indifferent to using and exploring this food. Ever since the Middle Ages we have been known throughout the world as a nation of meat eaters, an astounding irony for an island people. We have a few national delicacies recognized rightly as such abroad and they are mostly smoked fish. And it was these same fish and much the same ways of curing, salting and smoking them to preserve them throughout the winter that prehistoric man used on these same beaches. It is a telling thought to consider that sometime between the fifth and fourth millennium BC, when Britain became an island, smoked fish would have been part of the diet. A food we would not find very palatable now as it was not until the later prehistoric period that salt was used in the diet. It was during the Iron Age that salting food, as a method of preservation, was used in the whole of western Europe on a large scale.

When the Romans invaded Britain they brought with them a whole new cuisine. They used wine, spices and herbs, they mixed eggs and flour with fish, they used hot spices from Africa and the Middle East. They also began oyster farms, which still exist, and popularized some fish ignored before like the red mullet. Their recipes for fish are as sophisticated as any today; their basic method of poaching a fish in court-bouillon remains an unchanged classic, though we would perhaps find a sauce for boiled fish which contained honey, wine, vinegar, onion, pepper, lovage, parsley, oregano and liquamen (see page 145) too bewildering. Yet, if you try it, the flavour is intensely savoury and wholly delightful, but go easy on the honey in case it swamps the herbs with sweetness.

But like their architecture, Roman methods of cooking fish were soon forgotten when the Empire waned, not that they would have much affected the peasant class anyway, who would have continued to boil or bake the fish and eat it with sea salt.

Fish as a food got its bad name from being the food eaten on fast days and Fridays. Fish as punishment was not likely to be enjoyed, or sought out on days which were not fast days. Fish was also eaten by people too poor to eat meat. Thus fish suffered from two stigmas. There appears to be still a residue of this traditional feeling, though why it should linger here and not on the Continent I cannot say.

Because there were so many fast days, not only Fridays, but Saturdays and Wednesdays and the whole of Lent, the fishing industry grew and with it the recipes for the rich. The poor had to subsist on salt fish, potatoes and cereal, while by the Middle Ages, the rich were tucking into fish dishes on fast days which were as complicated as the Roman recipes before them. There seemed to be no regard for fish needing separate cooking from meat, or hardly any cooking at all; fish was cooked with fruit and spices in flour and water crusts or puréed into jellies.

It was in the Middle Ages that the herring came into its own. In Shetland the young herring with little oil was wind dried, but the fat oily herrings caught off the coast of East Anglia, fished in huge numbers, were salted and pickled. Yarmouth was the centre of the industry and the Yarmouth herring is still considered a great delicacy. Herrings were smoked as early as the thirteenth century. Soaked first in a heavy brine and then hung up in specially constructed chimneys, this was the red herring, the main sustenance of the poor for many years. The source of our use of red herring derives from the fact that a red herring was drawn across a fox's path to destroy its scent and mislead the hounds. We must surmise that the red herring had a powerful stench. You can still buy red herrings occasionally, but the one I tried a few years ago, was a feeble thing, with no smell and hardly any flavour.

The larger white fish were either boiled in salt water, or in wine and water and sometimes ale and water. It could be served with a green sauce of fresh pounded green herbs and garlic, thickened with breadcrumbs. Shellfish would be eaten by the rich and boiled, their liquor made into a sauce, often sweetened with honey or sugar and thickened with almonds, though the recipe for mussels is simpler and resembles that familiar and delicious *moules marinières* (see page 150). Large fish – swordfish, sturgeon, porpoise and whale – were also eaten, boiled or baked and quite often marinated in vinegar, herbs and salt to tenderize the tougher fish.

After the Reformation, fast days gradually lost their hold upon the people, though it was a slow waning. It was not until the Commonwealth that fish days were officially abolished as a papist institution; when the Restoration came fish had become scarce and expensive. Besides, the poor had at last turned against fish, salted, preserved and stewed to rags, and were happier to consume the poorer cuts of meat. So the fishing industry declined.

Yet new fish were being imported from the Mediterranean; pickled anchovies became popular in Elizabeth's reign and that ancestor of our taramasalata, botargo, a purée made from salted mullet roe, was eaten with great enjoyment by Pepys. The potential of the anchovy was quickly seen by cooks, and its strong flavour used in many dishes.

The next revolution in the eating of fish began with the discovery of containers that would keep the fish packed in ice so that it could travel. This began in the eighteenth century when salmon could be carried from Scotland to London. The method was suggested by a man from the East India Company who had been impressed in China by the way they carried fish packed around in snow.

Yet keeping fish fresh enough to be consumed with enjoyment was the biggest problem. The fish market in London was Billingsgate, near to the river, so that fishing smacks from East Anglia, Kent and Sussex could reach it easily. But fishmongers were notorious for their trickery in disguising rotting fish and pumping water into shellfish to make them weigh more.

The recipes up to the nineteenth century still abound with heavily spiced and sweet sauces which must have helped to disguise an old fish. It was in the eighteenth century that fish and meat were taken both together in the same meal, when the fish course preceded the meat, and when the idea of fish fast days were only observed by Roman Catholics. From this time at least, and especially in country parishes as in Parson Woodforde's table, fish were enjoyed for their freshness and delicacy of flavour. Simple fish recipes now start to appear, in which the fish was not overcooked or swamped in sauces, but plainly grilled with a herb butter, or poached to perfection and served with a mayonnaise.

Today we suffer an embarrassment of riches; there is so much fish to choose from. There is frozen fish, but there is also reconstituted fish, prepared, flaked and covered in sauces, there are fish soups, frozen fish pies, crab sticks, fish fingers and cakes, all of it tasting of additives to give the poor little fish flesh some semblance of flavour, and the fish dishes tasting very much like any other dish that comes away from the food manufacturer's hands. These should be given a wide berth. We allow over 3000 different additives to food, some of which are banned by the EEC. The French allow only seven in their food. When too many people suffer from allergic responses to food, when the relationship to diet and disease is recognizably clear, when junk food is one of the main source factors in this trend, then all convenience food should be strictly avoided.

This still leaves us with an embarrassment of riches. For the fresh fish throughout the year are numerous. Many too are cheap and an excellent meal can be made which costs little but which is nutritionally rich.

This book is to help you use and enjoy fish of all seasons. However strange the fish might seem upon the counter, you should find them within these pages. But not only are the rare fish here, there are also all our most popular and traditional favourites, with, I hope, new ways of cooking them.

This book did not set out to collect all the great classical fish recipes. But it deals with all the fish you are likely to find and others you can ask for, and the recipes on the whole are simple and quick but none the worse for that. For the secret of fish cooking is in the brevity of it. I have on the rare occasion fallen for the classic recipe and given it; *sole véronique* is an example, because it was one of the first great fish dishes I ever cooked, and I still recall that sweet taste of the white muscatel grape with the delicate sole and what a shocking revelation the combination was. It proves that now and again the most disparate ingredients fuse to perfection. This book aims to tell you what the fish are and to note briefly what cooking methods are best for it. The book also gives a recipe or two for each fish.

At the fishmongers, do not be timid. Ask questions and be ready to experiment. Make a friend of your fishmonger and get his advice and help. If he is any good, he will always order any fish for you that he has not yet stocked. He will also try and get you the exact size you want, and prepare the fish for you, so that that chore can be avoided – though there is great benefit in having fish heads, skin and bones, for the stock and soups.

Fish is the food for health; we should be eating far more of it. This book aims to encourage you to do that and to enjoy fish in all its variety without that ubiquitous mound of chips.

CHAPTER I

PREPARING
AND
COOKING FISH

'Good cooking is not elaboration – it is good simplicity.'
Dorothy Hartley, *Food in England*, (1954)

NUTRITION

Fish is an important source of high quality protein and minerals. Because its fatty acids are high in polyunsaturated fat, it is the best protein for slimmers. Fish contain phosphorus and iodine, the ones with tiny bones are also an excellent source of calcium. Fish are particularly rich in the B vitamins and they are almost free of carbohydrates.

The oilier fish are more nutritious than the white fish and the shellfish. Sardines, cockles, whelks and oysters contain as much iron, weight for weight, as beef. Eels are tremendously rich sources of vitamins A and D. Oysters contain vitamin C.

The cooking of fish, because it is simple and quick, will not induce any noticeable loss of the nutritional value. Grilling, baking and frying will make little difference. Poaching the fish will also ensure no loss of food value if the liquor is used as a sauce or soup.

FRESHNESS

Fish eaten the day it is caught has a wholly different flavour from when it is eaten two or three days afterwards. However, most of us cannot eat fish as fresh as this all the time. Fish are generally a few days old when they are bought and so they should be eaten on the day. Watch for the signs of freshness. Bright eyes, red gills, firmly attached scales. They ought to smell of the sea and not pong, their flesh should look white, their exterior markings clear, they should feel firm and not limp. Shellfish should feel heavy. If large and light, they have not grown into their shells. Plautus put the subject of freshness in fish well, when he remarked that 'Both fish and guests in three days are stale'.

COOKING

Fish need the minimum amount of cooking, enough heat to coagulate the protein and turn it white. Fish are never tough, except for octopus (see page 132) but overcooking will dry out the fish and make it chewy. You might just as well give it to the cat if it is at that stage. Precise details about cooking each fish are given in the text.

PREPARING FISH

All good fishmongers will prepare the fish for you and fillet it in the way you require. But it is not a difficult skill to acquire yourself.

1.   Scale the fish by laying it on a board, holding it by the tail and with the blade of a blunt knife scrape the scales away. They may fly off wildly, so some people prefer to do this task in the sink, so that the scales fall downwards. Rinse the fish under cold water.

2.   Gut the fish by slitting the belly below the head open, draw out the guts and rinse under cold running water.

3.   Skin the fish by drawing the head back and pulling it downwards. When you reach the fins, cut them and their bones free and draw them out; the skin can come off the fish like a glove if you use the head as a lever. If you want the head to stay on the fish, then cut the skin below the head and ease a corner away from one side, then pull it down, one side at a time. It is generally easier to start at the head end and move down to the tail.

4.   To fillet a fish. After it has been gutted and skinned, use a sharp pointed knife and cut as near to the backbone as is possible with one strong motion from head to tail. Do this on both sides and then ease the flesh away. Turn the fish over and do the same with the other side.

Flat fish are easier to prepare and fillet than round fish, but the procedure is similar. However, we often keep the heads on flat fish and they are not so necessary to use as a lever to get the skin off. Slice behind the head and start pulling the skin away; a pair of pliers is useful and makes the operation much easier. Flat fish have no scales to speak of. If the skin is left on the small ones, it should be pierced at the backbone, or else the fish will curl up when it is cooking. Pierce the skin down the length of the backbone before rolling in seasoning flour for frying.

EQUIPMENT

Wooden boards and sharp knives, these are the first essentials. But kitchen knives are personal objects and we all have our favourites. I would choose a cleaver, a filleting knife, a thin, sharp probe, a small knife and a thick short one for lifting the fillets. An oyster or a clam knife is useful if you eat shellfish frequently and, certainly if you are a crab lover, it is worth buying the tools for extracting the meat from the claws. The same tools are applicable to lobsters, though you will also need a light mallet to crack the claws.

Most of the cooking equipment can be adapted from what is already in the kitchen. A baking tin covered in foil can stand in as a fish kettle. But once you have started to fall in love with fish cooking, you will also want to get some of the equipment.

A large fish kettle is useful. Certainly for salmon, salmon trout and large sea fish, it ensures that the poaching is done efficiently and that the fish is not overcooked.

A Chinese wok can stand in for a steamer and for quick frying. A large copper frying pan will fry fish quickly and evenly. Most kitchens will have the following, all of which are useful in fish cookery: perforated spoons, fish slices, masses of cooking foil and greaseproof paper, wire meshes for straining, a food processor with all its various blades and gadgets (I now tend to put all the fresh herbs in the bowl of the processor and let the blade do the work for me), a pair of strong hinged tongs.

FROZEN FISH

Before I wrote this book I did not feel as strongly on this subject as I do now. I thought of frozen fish as the next best thing to fresh and in fact that is still roughly true. A lot of the fish which seem fresh in our shops have been frozen in the North Sea on the trawlers immediately after it is caught. This does not appear to harm the fish, though I am sure the flavour if cooked on board would be different.

The significant factor is the length of time the fish is frozen, for freezing fish does more than just preserve it. The low temperature breaks down the fibre, the collagen, which changes its structure and thus changes the flavour. It loses moisture, vitamins and minerals, which is why frozen fish can be so wet, flabby and flavourless. This fish is good for fish pies, fish cakes or croquettes, but not much else.

When shellfish are frozen, the fibre being more delicate still, the disastrous effect is more noticeable. The longer the fish is frozen the more it will deteriorate. Frozen crawfish from North America, for example, is sometimes seen in our supermarkets labelled lobster; the flesh has been reduced to a pink watery wool which can hardly be called a food.

The connective tissue of fish is a great deal less than in land animals, because the water they swim in supports them. The connective tissue is called collagen and this, when cooked, changes into gelatin.

George Lassalle in *The Adventurous Fish Cook* confuses gelatin with pectin and talks of some fish being high in pectin. Pectin is a carbohydrate found only in plants.

METHODS OF COOKING FISH

Grilling

Whole fish, cutlets or steaks are buttered or oiled and placed under a low or medium grill. Fish need only the minimum amount of cooking so it is best to hover about the stove. The grill base can be covered in foil and the fish should be turned once. The juices which are caught beneath the fish can be served with it or they can be mixed into a sauce. Grilled fish are often served with herb butters (see page 165). The size and thickness of the fish will naturally dictate how long it needs to be beneath the grill. Flat fish will take only a few minutes on each side. The test of when a fish is cooked through is when the flesh comes away easily from the central bone. If there is any doubt, stick the point of the knife into the flesh next to the bone and see whether it falls away easily. Approximate cooking times for each fish are given in the menus. Fish cooked *en brochette* can also be grilled (see Barbecuing).

Frying

Whole fish, cutlets or steaks can be deep or shallow fried.

SHALLOW FRIED: Use oil or butter or a mixture of both. If the temperature is going to be high, which for frying it generally is, use sunflower or corn oil which has a higher flash point. Both butter and olive oil will burn and ruin the flavour, though if you need the flavour of either olive oil or butter, mix whichever you choose with the corn or sunflower oil which will prevent it from burning.

The fish can be rolled in seasoned flour, oats, breadcrumbs or egg and breadcrumbs before frying. The fish can also be dipped into batter, although that is a method generally associated with deep frying.

DEEP FRYING: Use corn or sunflower oil and bring the oil up to the required temperature before immersing the fish. Most cookery books mention a blue haze or slight smoke on the surface of the oil which is an indication of the temperature. A safer method is to drop into the oil a particle of food, such as a drop of batter or even a small crouton, to see whether it starts to cook. This is a safer method as if the oil is beginning to smoke it is almost at flash point.

The larger the pieces of fish the longer they will need to cook. If they are in batter they are done when the batter has turned golden brown. Small fish balls in batter are also best deep-fried, as the spheres will cook evenly. Shallow frying tends to flatten the sides.

Never use blended vegetable oil as this is high in saturated fats. It is the cheapest oil and is used in the majority of fish and chip shops and hotels. Never use the same oil more than twice and pour the oil through muslin after it has cooled to get rid of food particles and impurities. Some people use the oil a third or even fourth time, this may be all right if the cooking is done within two or three days but the oil can easily take on a jaded flavour which will spoil the fish.

A deep-frying pan with basket is an essential utensil if there is going to be a lot of deep frying. But it is a coarse way of cooking fish and tends to be fattening. I cannot recommend it except on a very few occasions. The utensil that then can be used is a wok which will take one large piece of fish or two medium sized steaks. It is also, because of the bowl shape, highly economical in the amount of oil used.

It is the soft white fish which deep fry the best: cod, hake, haddock and whiting.

TYPES OF BATTER

English Batter

50g (2oz) wholemeal flour
25g (1oz) plain flour
pinch of salt

1 egg
150ml (¼pt) milk

Make a well in the flour and salt and break in the egg. Make a paste and then add the milk slowly. Beat with a whisk, or place into a blender jar and whiz until you have a smooth and frothy mixture. Leave for an hour and beat or whiz again immediately before using. This makes a thick batter; if it is too thick, add a couple of tablespoons of water. You can also separate the egg, whisk in the white and beat that into the batter. This will make a lighter batter.

Japanese Batter

100g (4oz) plain flour
1 egg

150ml (¼pt) iced water

Mix everything together to a smooth consistency. This makes a very light batter. Again, you can separate the egg, beat the white until it is stiff and mix it in. This is Japanese tempura used for covering vegetables. It is good with cubes of fish.

Greek Batter

100g (4oz) plain flour
1 teaspoon baking powder
1 egg
1 tablespoon olive oil
1 tablespoon ouzo *or* pernod

150ml (¼pt) water
1 tablespoon chopped fennel
    leaves
pinch of salt

Beat, whisk or blend all the ingredients until you have a smooth and frothy consistency. Leave for 1 hour and beat again before use.

Indian Batter

100g (4oz) chick pea (gram) flour
1 teaspoon baking powder
1 teaspoon curry powder

1 egg
150ml (¼pt) water
1 tablespoon corn oil

Mix as for the above batters.

Griddling

This method of cooking is more common on the continent. It is much used in Spain for the cooking of shellfish where *Gambas a la Plancha* means prawns cooked on the hot plate. The prawns are soaked in a marinade of oil and lemon juice, they are then placed on a flat iron plate over a fire and brushed with more oil and lemon as they are cooked.

The iron plate can be flat or ribbed; if the latter the fish will be marked with diagonal scorch marks. No oil is used on the plate but the fish must be lightly oiled before cooking. Flat or ribbed cooking pans can be bought and used on an electric or gas ring. It is a good method of cooking for large shellfish and firm meaty fish that are rich in their own oils like tunny and the mackerel family.

Steaming

There are various steamers on the market but most of them are made for vegetables and will be too small for fish. Recently there have been steamers made to contain larger fish, though they are not always widely available. (Appendix II). Fish cooks tend to improvise when they wish to steam fish, indeed there is not one distinguished fish cookery book that can not resist telling the story of Brillat-Savarin's method with the steamed turbot. The turbot was too big for any possible cooking utensil so he used a wash tub and a wine rack. This seems to be going too far, but anything that will lift the fish from the court-bouillon and contain the steam will work

An ordinary fish kettle can be used if the rack stands on something so that the fish is well above the court-bouillon. George Lassalle in *The Adventurous Fish Cook* recommends an asparagus kettle in which the fish are steamed head downwards. If you have a wok with a lid then you can steam a fairly large fish by placing it on a rack inside the wok. Another Chinese method is to use the dim sum steamers, where several smaller fish can be steamed at one time.

To get the value from steaming it is best to use a court-bouillon with the addition of wine, or a strongly flavoured fish fumet. (See Chapter VII & Glossary).

Baking

There are three methods of baking, with butter, with stock or *en papillote*.

WITH BUTTER: This is done by smearing a baking tin liberally with seasoned butter and spreading more on top of the fish and baking in a medium oven at 350°F/180°C/Gas Mark 4 for approximately 20 minutes. The size of the fish and whether it is stuffed or not will dictate the exact time. A three- to four-pound fish which has been stuffed will need a good 45 minutes. The butter can often be augmented with a glass of white wine, dry sherry or vermouth, a small amount (3 tablespoons) of fish fumet can also be added. Fresh or dried herbs can be sprinkled over the fish. This method is akin to grilling and in many cases is somewhat easier, as the cook does not have to hover over the stove. But the cooking must be carefully timed, or else the fish will become too dry and in the last resort actually burn. Oily fish like herrings and mackerel can be baked without the addition of butter.

WITH STOCK: The fish is placed in a baking tin with a stock which can be a fumet or a vegetable stock with the addition of finely chopped vegetables. There is no need to cover the fish though it must not dry out. The fish is cooked, partly poached in the stock, partly steamed and partly baked. It is an excellent method with the larger flat fish: turbot, halibut and brill.

EN PAPILLOTE: This is an oiled parcel of greaseproof paper which encloses fish with butter and herbs. The parcel is then baked in the oven and opened at the table. All the aroma and flavour is kept in until that moment. This method of cooking is now more usually done with foil and we tend to refer to the method simply as baking with foil. It is a very useful method with large fish which are too big to go into a fish kettle to be poached. Salmon, turbot, sea bass can all be cooked in buttered foil, baked in the oven.

Barbecuing

Very large fish can be laid straight on to a grill over a charcoal fire. The difficulty comes when the fish has to be turned so that it can be cooked on both sides; you will then need more than one person and several implements. However, it is a rare occurrence when a very large fish is cooked in this manner. For the more normally sized fish, there are fish shaped wire clamps which hold the fish firm so that they can be turned with ease.

The charm of barbecuing is to cook the fish so that the skin is crisp and slightly charred. The main flaw in barbecuing is the ease with which the food can be turned into a cinder and fish, because it needs the minimum amount of cooking, can easily be blackened and spoiled.

EN BROCHETTE: Small chunks of fish marinated in oil and lemon are threaded on a skewer or barbecue spit, with or without the addition of vegetables such as mushrooms, onions, green or red peppers and tomato. The brochette is cooked over the barbecue fire and can easily be turned. One of the best fish is the angler fish or monk fish which will take on a flavour of green pepper if it is used (see **grilling**).

Smoking

There are commercial smokers of many different sizes which can now be purchased (see Appendix II). This is a method of hot smoking which cooks the fish rather than preserves it. The fish is lightly salted for an hour, it is then laid on a rack in the box, sawdust is put beneath the rack and covered with a tin plate, the lid is placed on the box so that it is air tight. A flame is put beneath the box and the fish cooks in the smoke of the smouldering sawdust. It is done within 10 to 15 minutes. It can be eaten immediately or left to grow cold. Fish done this way is delicious, it is unlike cold smoked fish and for the fish lover a home smoker is essential. Pâtés and mousses made from these smoked fish are also delicious.

Marinating

This is strictly not a form of cooking, yet it is a method of changing the molecular structure of the fish by the action of acid, either lemon juice or vinegar. The fish may still seem raw, yet it will have changed colour, be tender, have its full flavour and be easily digested. The prepared fish should be filleted and cut into small slices. It should remain in the marinade for at least 12 hours, and a whole day will not do it any harm. Indeed I consider that most fish can remain in the marinade for as long as a week if kept in the refrigerator. However, marinated fish is at its peak after 24 hours.

All marinades should contain sugar, salt, cider or wine, lemon juice or vinegar, herbs or spices. Various recipes for marinades are given in the book.

There is a Latin American dish Caveach which uses this method of cooking. The fish (any white fish will do) is sliced and put into a marinade mostly of lime juice which is spiced with hot chillies. To this are added onions, sliced peppers and pickles. This dish is sometimes called Ceviche. It is descended from another dish called Escoveitch which crops up in the West Indies. There the fish is rubbed with lime juice then deep fried then put into a pickle of vinegar and hot peppers. This dish in turn originated in southern Spain and France where it is called Escabeche or Scaveech or Caveach. It is thought that Catsup was derived from Caveach.

I prepared for a summer luncheon party a variation of the dish. I home-smoked a dog fish and left it to cool. I took the bone from the flesh and sliced it, I added a thinly sliced green and yellow pepper and on a large platter arranged fish and peppers. Between I scattered some freshly boiled kernels from two sweetcorn and some peeled broad beans. Around the sides were some freshly boiled prawns and shrimps. Over this I poured the juice of two limes mixed with a tablespoon of olive oil, a teaspoon of tabasco and a teaspoon of green peppercorns. The dish was a great success, even with small children, who mopped up the juices with bread.

Poaching

Fish used to be cooked in salt water and still is occasionally for some varieties, as on page 56. However, this may work very well on a trawler in the North Sea but it is a crude way of cooking the fish and it can easily overcook it. Instead of brine a flavoured stock is used which is called a court-bouillon. The vegetables and spices are simmered together for half an hour, it is then sieved, poured back into the pan and the fish is lowered into it for the required time.

Basic Court-Bouillon

1.25l (2pt) water	1 tablespoon black peppercorns
600ml (1 pt) dry cider or white wine	1 tablespoon pickling spices
	2 carrots, sliced
2 tablespoons white wine vinegar or lemon juice	2 onions, sliced
	Bunch of parsley stalks
1 bouquet garni	½ teaspoon salt

Bring everything to the boil. Simmer for 45 minutes to an hour, then drain all the bits out of the stock.

Immerse the fish in the hot court-bouillon, bring it back to simmering point, ensure that there is a tight fitting lid on the pan, turn off the heat and leave the fish for 20 minutes (see salmon and salmon trout on pages 80 and 82).

The court-bouillon, once it has had the fish cooked in it becomes a fish fumet; this is often reduced by boiling and becomes a basis for soups, stews and sauces.

WHAT TO DRINK WITH FISH

There has long been a rule that you must only drink dry white wine with fish. Rules are made to be broken. Red wine can make a stunning complement to some fish, though it reacts sharply with shellfish and the tannin can taste almost abrasive. So I would avoid red wine with shellfish but a well chilled rosé goes down a treat.

A good Gewurztraminer is often drunk with oysters or smoked salmon, and that smoky green bouquet can be delicious; though champagne is thought to be the classic combination, I always find bubbles and food are not the happiest of marriages.

Any of the Sauvignon wines made from the Blanc Fumé grape are a beautiful foil also to shellfish, as is Muscadet or one of the Alsatian wines – a dish of scallops for example can even take a slightly medium dry wine.

For white fish, I would choose a Sauvignon, Chardonnay, Chablis or a dry Californian white. A Macon or, more expensively, a Pouilly Fuissé, Pouilly Fumé, or Meursault is for a celebration dinner, though why one cannot have these every day, I don't know (expense being the only factor to stop us). Dry Italian whites, like Verdicchio, are perfect with white fish and that very pleasant Swiss wine, Fendant.

Smoked fish, like haddock, eel or trout, need a sharper wine to cut through the oiliness – a Bourgogne Aligoté for example, a Chenin Blanc, or a Vinho Verde or white Rioja, or the white wines made from the black grape, such as Pinot Noir Blanc, or the pinkish Vin Gris.

It is the more robust fish, like tunny, swordfish, and red mullet, also the dishes which have strong flavours, which can happily demand a red wine. A chilled Beaujolais, Côtes du Rhone, Chianti, Valpolicella, or a Corbières, a Rioja or a Dão red. The stronger tasting a dish, the more powerful the red wine can be.

CHAPTER II

SEA FISH

'A man may fish with the worm that hath eat of a king, and eat of the fish that hath fed of that worm.'

William Shakespeare, *Hamlet*, IV, iii, 29

Angler Fish or Monkfish

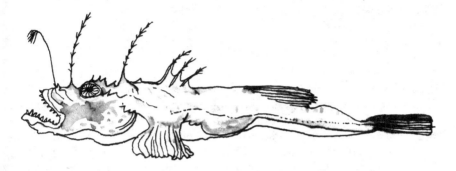

This beautiful fish is becoming more and more available as it becomes more fashionable. It is only beautiful in flavour for its appearance, which you never see in the fishmongers (as only the tail is displayed), comes out of Bosch's vision of Hell.

It is a deep-water fish caught in British fishing grounds and is in season all the year round.

The fish is confused by most people with the angel fish or angel shark which is also called monkfish. *

The fish can grow to 2m (6½ft) in length but only the tail of the angler fish is eaten which has a central backbone and no other smaller ones. It is said that some restaurants cook the flesh beneath sauces and allow it to masquerade as scampi or even lobster. The fish can be baked, casseroled, fried, grilled, poached or smoked. It is excellent *en brochette* with peppers and mushrooms and then barbecued or grilled. It also smokes beautifully. It is a fish that will adapt itself to almost any form of cooking and will take very strong flavours.

*So serious is this confusion that numerous fish guides and cookery books make the error. Safeway's *Fish Guide* and *The Sunday Times Complete Cook Book* are but two examples. They give a picture of the angel shark while referring to the flesh of the angler fish. The angel shark is caught and eaten in the Mediterranean countries. I have never eaten it so cannot compare the flavour with the angler fish. It spends the winter in deep waters and the summer in shallow, inshore waters, where the female produces 10–25 young. Compare this to the angler fish where the female lays one million eggs. The annual European catch of the angler fish is 35,000 tons, Britain takes only 3,500 tons while Spain take 13,000 and France 14,000. The angler fish is referred to in fishmongers in Britain as monkfish, in France it is *lotte*, in Spain, *rape*.

Lotte Provençal

1 piece of angler fish weighing
   1.25kg (2½lb)
675g (1½lb) tomatoes
150ml (¼pt) olive oil
2 onions, finely chopped
5 cloves garlic, crushed

generous handful each, chopped
   parsley and basil
2 tablespoons tomato purée
12 stoned black olives
sea salt and black pepper

Peel and seed the tomatoes, chop them coarsely. Pour the oil into a large casserole and cook the tomatoes, onions and garlic over a low heat for about 30 minutes. Add the herbs and tomato purée and cook for a few minutes more until you have a thick sauce. Place the fish in one piece in the sauce and bake in a preheated oven 350°F/180°C/Gas Mark 4 for 40 minutes. Take the fish out, place on a platter and cover with the olives, pour the sauce around the fish and carve pieces from it.

Roulade de Lotte

225g (8oz) angler fish
225g (8oz) puff pastry (frozen
   will do)
100g (4oz) mozzarella cheese
2 tbsp sorrel purée made from
   25g (1oz) butter and 10 sorrel
   leaves (use spinach if no sorrel
   available)

generous handful of parsley, well
   chopped
poppy seeds
sea salt and freshly ground black
   pepper
a little melted butter

Bone the fish and slice it thinly so that it is about 5mm (¼in) in thickness. Roll the pastry out so that it is a thin rectangle. Trim the edges. Dice the mozzarella into tiny cubes and mix them with the sorrel or spinach purée. Season the purée and the fish. Spread the purée over the pastry so that it comes to about 1cm (½in) from the edges. Lay the fish on top and sprinkle the parsley over the fish. Roll up very gently from the outside patting the filling down as you turn the pastry over. Brush the top with melted butter and sprinkle with a little sea salt and a few poppy seeds. Place on an oiled baking tray and place in a preheated oven at 400°F/200°C/Gas Mark 6 for 30 minutes.

Angler can also be substituted in the following recipes:
Caveach, page 21
Cod Steaks with Lemon Sauce, page 32
Fish Simmered in Ginger and Soy Sauce, page 39

**With plainly grilled, fried or baked angler, most of the herb butters,
mayonnaises and sauces in Chapter IX are suitable.**

Bass

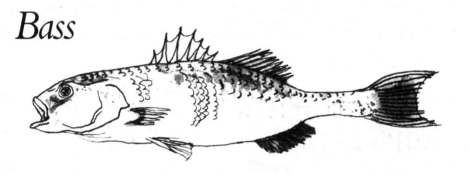

In season June to March. Depending on size can be cooked various ways: if
large, 1.5kg (2½lbs) or over, by baking or barbecueing; if small, grill or
barbecue; when very large, steaks can be cut from the fish and fried or grilled.
The fishmonger will fillet the fish, or cut the steaks from it. But it is commonly bought whole and frequently stuffed. Sauces: Orange, Bresse Bleu,
Provençal. You can sometimes find another fish, the striped bass or rock fish,
which is a cousin of the sea bass. A beautiful fish with the characteristic dense
white flesh, the fishmonger will fillet it or cut steaks from it. Use any of the
recipes for angler fish or treat as below.

Baked Bass

1.25–1.5kg (2½–3lb) prepared
   sea bass
3 tablespoons olive oil
4 cloves garlic chopped
handful of chopped parsley and
   tarragon

juice and zest from one lemon
1 glass of dry white wine
sea salt and freshly ground black
   pepper
25g (1oz) wholemeal
   breadcrumbs

The simplest method when the fish is very fresh. Put a little of the oil in a baking tray, lay the cleaned fish down in it, fill the cavity with the chopped garlic and herbs, brush the top with the rest of the oil and pour the lemon juice, zest and white wine over the fish. Sprinkle with salt and pepper and the breadcrumbs. Place in a preheated oven at 400°F/200°C/Gas Mark 6 for 30 minutes. Baste with the oil and juices half way through the cooking.

Bass steaks can also be substituted in the following recipes:
Flounder à la Deauvillaise, pages 41–2
Dory in Cider and Cream, pages 51–2
Plaice with Coriander Butter, page 56
Turbot with Crab Sauce, page 66
Flétan au Poivre, page 48
Whole bass can be stuffed and baked as in the grey mullet (pages 43–4), hake (pages 46–7), and haddock (page 45) recipes.
Poached or steamed bass goes well with most of the herb butters, mayonnaises and sauces in Chapter IX.

Ray's Bream

This fish can be found in the spring and summer all along the south coast of England. It can grow up to 70cm (28in) and its flesh is faintly pink and is composed of long strings like the family of rays, yet it is part of the bream family. It is very common in Spanish waters and in Western Africa, but is not often caught in the Mediterranean or in British waters. Yet it is delicious to eat and should be poached in a court-bouillon with the addition of wine and then eaten with a sauce or mayonnaise. Large specimens can be baked in foil with a herb butter. They can also be filleted and cooked like skate.

Brill

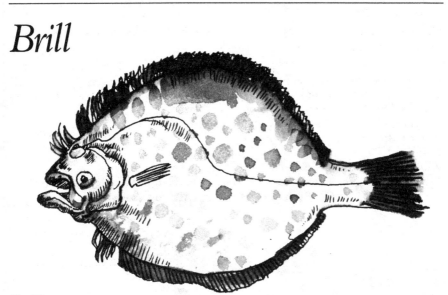

Not widely available although in season all the year round. It can grow to 60cm (2ft) but is most often seen at half that size. Occasionally you may come across the large ones when they are sold like turbot and halibut in steaks. Buy them if you ever see them as they are one of the best flavoured of the flat fish, lagging not far behind Dover sole or turbot. If the fish is large enough get it filleted and use any of the recipes for the flat fish. Otherwise grill them with a little herb butter or as in the recipe below.

Grilled Brill with Anchovy Sauce

Allow one fish for each person   A little butter

For the sauce

25g (1oz) butter   freshly ground black pepper
25g (1oz) flour   2 tablespoons lemon juice
300ml (½pt) vegetable stock   1 tin anchovies or
2 tablespoons double cream   2 tablespoons of anchovy
1 egg yolk   essence

Lightly butter the fish and place under a low grill while you make the sauce. Melt the butter in a pan, add the flour and make a roux. Slowly add the stock to make a smooth thin sauce. Mix the cream and egg yolk together in a bowl, add a little of the hot sauce, stirring thoroughly, then pour it back into the pan. Cook over a gentle heat adding the pepper and the lemon juice. Drain the tin

of anchovies and mash them to a purée, add them (or the anchovy essence) to
the sauce and mix thoroughly.

Brill can also be substituted in the following recipes:
Grilled Dab with Tarragon Butter, page 38
Filets de Sole Véronique, pages 40–41
Flounder à la Deauvillaise, pages 41–42
Plaice with Coriander Butter, page 56
Skate with Capers, page 62
Whiting in Herb Sauce, page 68
The sweetness of brill needs a gentle sauce or herb butter: Parsley, Lemon or
Crab Butter (page 167), Bechamel, Mornay or Shrimp Sauce (pages 170–74).

Bonito

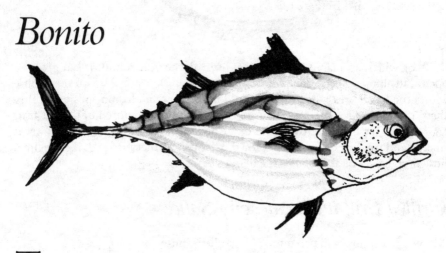

The only member of the tunny and mackerel family whose habitat encircles
the British Isles. It can grow up to 90cm (3ft) and is excellent to eat. It may be
caught in British waters all the year round, but is not often seen in the
fishmongers. It can be bought in steaks, when it can be dipped into seasoned
flour and fried in butter and olive oil. It is a popular fish in Spain and Portugal
and one of the most famous recipes comes from the Basque region.

In Japan, bonito is cut into strips, and dried and used to make stocks or
dashi; this is a basic soup stock which can be bought in Japanese stores.
Japanese dried bonito is sold in two forms, one which resembles a block of dry
wood, and the other which is grated and is called *hanagatsu*. This will make a
good, well flavoured fish stock if you add the grated bonito to 25g (1oz) of
kombu seaweed to 900ml (1½pt) water, bring to the boil and simmer for 5
minutes, then sieve and use for soups or sauces.

Marmite

450g (1lb) fresh bonito steaks
150ml (¼pt) olive oil
2 dried red chillis
2 large onions, chopped
6 cloves garlic
2 red peppers, cored and sliced

675g (1½lb) potatoes
1 teaspoon paprika
sea salt and black pepper
1.25l (2pt) fish fumet (see page
  145)

In a large marmite or casserole pour in the oil, add the red chillis, the chopped onions and the fish. Crush the garlic over the fish and add the chopped red peppers. Peel the potatoes, chop them coarsely and add them. Sprinkle them with paprika, sea salt and black pepper. Pour in the fish fumet and bake in a preheated oven with the lid firmly on at 325°F/170°C/Gas Mark 3 for 3 hours. Take the marmite from the oven, give it a good stir and take out the red chillis before serving.

Cod

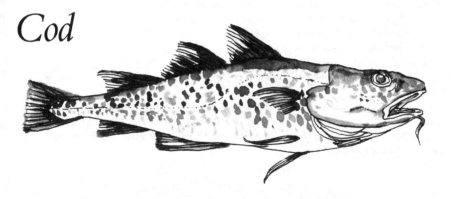

Available all the year round. Best if bought fresh from fishermen on the beach. These are the small inshore cod (codling) which are caught through the winter months. The flavour is quite different from the larger cod caught by deep sea trawling.

Cod adapts well to all forms of cooking. If fresh and young the simplest methods of cooking are best. Grill or bake in foil with butter and herbs. Excellent fried in batter or egg and breadcrumbed. The flesh is very white, flaky and succulent. If the fish is large it is sold in steaks. These are best grilled, baked or barbecued. Cod is especially good with cheese, tomato or lemon sauce.

Cod Steaks with Lemon Sauce

4 cod steaks (about 2.5cm [1 inch] thick)
50g (2oz) butter
25g (1oz) flour

300ml (½pt) fish fumet (see page 145)
juice and zest of 2 lemons
sea salt and black pepper
2 egg yolks

Melt the butter in a saucepan and brush some of it onto the cod steaks. Place the steaks under a hot grill for 3–5 minutes, turning once. Meanwhile make the sauce. Add the flour to the remaining butter to make a roux and cook the paste for a moment. Then add the fish fumet, the lemon juice and zest, season with salt and pepper and continue to cook, simmering quietly for 3–4 minutes. Beat the egg yolks in a small bowl, add a little of the hot sauce to them, stirring thoroughly, then pour the egg and sauce mixture back into the pan, and stir until the sauce thickens without it boiling. Take the skin from the fish and serve with the sauce beneath the steaks.

Cod can also be substituted in the following recipes:
Fish Simmered in Ginger and Soy Sauce, page 39
Poached Haddock with Mustard Sauce, pages 45–6
Plaice with Coriander Butter, page 56
Turbot with Crab Sauce, page 66
See also, French method with Whiting, page 68
Any of the batters on pages 17–18 can be used with cod for shallow or deep frying.
Use strong sauces with cod: Anchovy (page 170), Mussel (page 171), Curry (page 171), Mustard (page 171), Green Peppercorn (page 173) and Horseradish (page 174), as well as the more conventional Tomato, Parsley and Cheese Sauces (pages 170–71).

Cod Roes

These can be bought separately by weight in the fishmongers. They are generally sold in pairs as, if separated, the membrane will break. Handle them with care so that the membrane remains intact. They need to be simmered in salted boiling water for about ten minutes. Let them cook then drain them. They may now be kept in a refrigerator or in a cool place until you need to cook them. Cut them into slices about 1cm (½in) in depth, turn them in seasoned flour and then fry them in butter and oil until they are crisp. Serve them with any hot spicy sauce from pages 170–74. They make an excellent light supper dish. (See pages 116–17 for smoked cod roes).

Slices of fried cod roe go well with the following hot spicy sauces:
Anchovy (page 170), Curry (page 171), Mustard (page 171), Caper (page 173),
Green Peppercorn (page 173), Spiced (page 173), Hot Pepper (page 174),
Horseradish (page 174), and Hot Tomato (page 174).

Coley

In season all the year round. Often frozen in fillets. Much despised as only good for the cat, but its slightly off-putting grey flesh goes white in cooking. It is not a delicate fish, so it is best used in fish pies, or croquettes, or minced and used in a sauce, or as an ingredient in soups.

Fish Croquettes with Tomato Sauce

450g (1lb) coley fillets
50g (2oz) butter
450g (1lb) potatoes
1 tablespoon dried fennel
1 bunch of fresh green fennel (or parsley)

sea salt and freshly ground black pepper
one beaten egg
wholemeal breadcrumbs
oil for frying

For the sauce

450g (1lb) tomatoes
2 cloves garlic, crushed
fish liquor
25g (1oz) flour

25g (1oz) butter
sea salt and freshly ground black pepper

Melt the butter in a pan and add the coley fillets. Put a lid on the saucepan and let it sauté over a low heat until the fish is cooked through – about 5 minutes. Strain any liquor away and reserve for the sauce. Boil the potatoes, skin and mash them. Take any bones or skin from the fish. Crush the dried fennel and chop the green fennel or parsley. Mix all the ingredients well together. Season to taste. Add the beaten egg. Take out a little of the mixture and roll into croquette shapes. Then cover in breadcrumbs. Fry them briefly in a little oil until they are golden and crisp.

For the sauce

Place the tomatoes with the garlic in a saucepan, place the lid on the top and leave over a very low heat to cook in their own juice for about 10 minutes, then place everything into the blender and whiz for a moment. Sieve, throw away the skin and pips and add the reserved fish liquor to the tomato stock. Melt the butter in a pan, add the flour and make a roux, cook for a moment. Then add the tomato and fish stock to make a thin sauce. Taste and season.

Coley can be used in the following soups and fish pies:
Simple Fish Soup, page 146
Bouillabaisse, page 147
Bourride, page 147
White Fish Stew, page 152
Smoked Fish Stew, page 153
Sea Fish Pie, page 154
Fish Timbale, pages 155–6

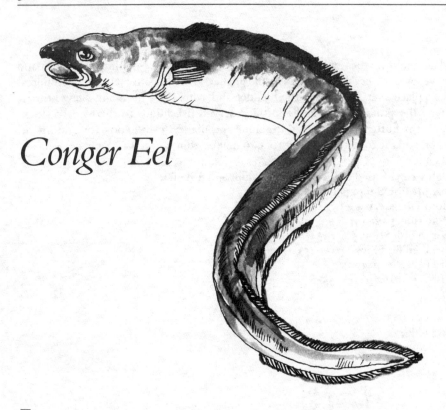

Conger Eel

In season March to October. Available in enterprising fish shops. Or can be bought from fishermen in south-west parts of England. Can grow up to 2.5m (8 feet) long with a circumference of 15cm (6 inches) at its fattest part. It is easily recognizable, as it is strongly reminiscent of the ancient name for it, the sea snake. Buy from the thickest part, behind the head, as the last part of the eel is a mass of bones and is only useful for stocks and soups.

It can be cooked baked in foil, casseroled in cider, or smoked. The fishmonger will take the tough black skin away from the steaks or the piece of eel that you choose, but it is not difficult to skin yourself. Peel a corner of the skin away, then use pliers to unpeel the skin like a glove. Cook the eel in steaks of 2.5cm (1 inch) thickness or in one large piece.

Roast Eel with Apples and Cider

Eel weighing 1.25kg (2½lb)
1 tablespoon flour
50g (2oz) butter
600ml (1pt) dry cider

sea salt and black pepper
450g (1lb) tart eating apples
2 tablespoons thick cream

Rub the flour into the fish, melt the butter in a large frying pan and brown the outside of the fish. Remove the fish from the pan, reserving the fat, and place in a baking tin. Pour three quarters of the cider over it, sprinkle it with pepper and salt and bake in a preheated oven at 400°F/200°C/Gas Mark 6 for 20 minutes, basting the fish with the cider. Test with a sharp knife to see if the fish is cooked through to the bone, if not, give it another 10 minutes. Meanwhile peel the apples, core them and cut into eighths. Fry them in the reserved butter for a few minutes until they are just crisp at the edges. Take the fish from the oven and place on a platter. Arrange the apple slices around the fish, pour the juices and cider from the tray into a pan and add the rest of the cider and boil fiercely to reduce by a third; you should have about 300ml (½pt) of liquid. Then add the cream, stirring until you have a smooth sauce. Pour over the fish and serve.

Large pieces of eel can also be cooked as in the baked stuffed fish recipes.
Small steaks of conger eel can be grilled with any of the herb butters (page 167)
or floured, egg and breadcrumbed and fried in butter. Other suitable recipes
are:
Fish Simmered in Ginger and Soy Sauce, page 37
Caveach, page 21
Garfish with Sauce Verte, pages 42–3
Or follow the routine for barbecued fish on page 71.
Smaller pieces of eel can be cooked *en brochette* and either grilled or
barbecued.
Sauces suitable are Crab (page 170), Anchovy (page 170), Curry (page 171),
Mustard (page 171), Herb (page 171), Fennel (page 171), Caper (page 173),
Walnut (page 174), and Hot Tomato (page 174).

Cuttlefish

Cuttlefish is a member of the cephalopod family which includes squid and octopus (see pages 136–8 and 132–3) and it is the most common in British waters. It is available all the year round, but you will rarely find it on sale. The only sign of its existence around the shores of Britain is the white cuttlefish bone that one frequently comes across on beaches. This used to be ground as tooth powder but is now usually found in bird cages. Cuttlefish has more ink in its sac than either the octopus or the squid. It makes very good eating and after being prepared can be grilled but is more commonly simmered in a stew.

There is a famous Italian dish where it is the main ingredient and the ink is used; *Cacciucco Livornese*. Jane Grigson, as a young girl, ate it one day at Viareggio and has never forgotten its ebony black appearance or its exquisite flavour.

Dab

Season from September to December. A member of the plaice family and often quite mistakenly despised. Large dabs can be filleted after being skinned, smaller ones may be cooked whole. If filleted, follow the recipes for other flat fish, especially plaice and lemon sole. If cooked whole, they are best floured or egg and breadcrumbed and fried in butter. The smaller fish have a delicate and sweet flavour.

Grilled Dab with Tarragon Butter

Allow 1 fish to each person
75g (3oz) butter
juice from ½ lemon

2 tablespoons fresh, chopped
    tarragon
sea salt and black pepper

Have the fishmonger skin the dabs on both sides. With a sharp knife cut into the flesh down the back bone to stop the fish curling under the heat. Mix the butter and lemon juice together then beat in the chopped tarragon. Smear a little of the butter onto each side of the fish and place under a medium grill for about 10 minutes. Serve the fish with more tarragon butter.

Dog Fish

These are more commonly known on the fishmonger's slab as rock eel, rock salmon or rock fish, they are also sometimes called catfish. They are a member of the shark family along with the monkfish and the skate (see pages 25–7 and 62–3). They are available all the year round and often found as one of the fish that is battered in the fried fish shop.

They make excellent eating and can be bought in cutlets or fillets, they have a dense white flesh and are high in gelatin, they are excellent in soups, stews and fish pies and are very good *en brochette*, barbecued with peppers, tomatoes and mushrooms. They can also be smoked after being salted but will also take well to being cooked, in the Breton fashion, with white wine, butter and cream. The good thing about the fish of the shark family, because of the quality of the flesh, is that one can cook them in an endless variety of ways. In the Far East, where the following recipe comes from, the treatment is entirely opposite to that in France.

Fish simmered in Ginger and Soy Sauce

4 fillets of dog fish
150ml (¼pt) water
150ml (¼pt) soy sauce

150ml (¼pt) saki
50g (2oz) ginger root, grated
1 tablespoon sugar

Pour the water and the rest of the ingredients except for the fish into a pan. Bring to the boil and simmer for 2–3 minutes. Lay the fish in the stock and continue to simmer over a low heat for 5–8 minutes. Take the fish out of the pan and keep warm, reduce the stock to a syrup, pour over the fish and serve.

This fish can be substituted in any of the recipes for angler fish, see page 26.
Also excellent in any of the soups, stews and fish pies in Chapter VII.
Can be poached and eaten hot or cold with any of the herb butters, mayonnaises and sauces in Chapter IX.

Dover Sole

In season all the year round. One of the great fish of the world that has inspired many cooks to create new recipes for it. It is best plainly grilled with butter and lemon, but I cannot resist giving one of the great classical recipes. Get the fishmonger to skin and fillet the sole for the recipe below.

Filets de Sole Véronique

8 fillets of sole (allowing 2 per person)
sea salt and black pepper
50g (2oz) butter
4 shallots, finely chopped
300ml (½pt) dry white wine

225g (8oz) seedless white muscatel grapes
2 egg yolks
3 tablespoons thick cream
more grapes for garnish

Salt and pepper the fillets and roll them up. Melt the butter in a casserole where the fillets will fit snugly and fry the shallots, for a moment or two. Reserve 85ml (3fl oz) of the wine and pour the rest over the shallots. Take the pan away from the heat and fit the fish in. Bake in a preheated over at 400°F/200°C/Gas Mark 6 for 15 minutes. Meanwhile heat the grapes in the reserved wine and let them simmer for a minute. Take the dish from the oven and pour the sauce into the pan with the grapes. Beat the egg yolks together in a bowl and add a little of the sauce to them, mixing well; return to the pan and let the sauce thicken without boiling and then add the cream, taste and check for seasoning. Carefully take out the fillets of sole from the casserole and arrange on a platter, pour the sauce around them. Decorate with more grapes by slicing them in half and arranging them on top of the fillets.

Can be substituted in:
Flounder à la Deauvillaise, pages 41–2

Flounder

In season all the year round. Another flat fish which likes to spend the summer months in river estuaries. About 30cm (12 inches) long and not often seen in the fishmongers. Should be eaten when very fresh, otherwise the flesh becomes increasingly tasteless. However, a large flat flounder will have a good firm white flesh. It will fillet well and all the recipes for other flat fish can be used. If very fresh it is best grilled, fried or steamed.

Another flounder also appears in our fishmongers called the witch flounder, pole dab or Torbay sole. All the recipes for other flat fish are applicable.

Flounder à la Deauvillaise

8 fillets of flounder
225g (8oz) onions
75g (3oz) butter
pinch of nutmeg

sea salt and black pepper
150ml (5fl oz) single cream
handful chopped parsley

Chop the onions finely and cook them in the butter over a low heat so that they go transparent. Add the nutmeg, salt and pepper. Roll the fillets of flounder and then lay them among the onions and place the dish in a preheated oven 350°F/180°C/Gas Mark 4 for 20 minutes. Carefully take out the fillets and place them on a warm platter. Add the cream and parsley to the onions and mix well. Let the sauce simmer for a moment before pouring over the fish, garnish with more parsley before serving.

See other recipes for flat fish and dover sole.

Garfish

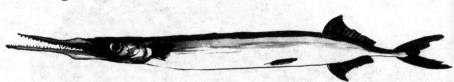

T his is a member of the eel family and can grow up to 70cm (2⅓ft). It is in season from September to June. Very popular in Denmark, it sometimes appears in English fishmongers where they will fillet it for you. It has not been popular as food because of its green skeleton which appears poisonous. This is in fact a harmless pigmentation and could be turned to your advantage by serving the fish in a *sauce verte* which would look appealing. The fillets are good to eat, but tend to be rather dry so the fish is best poached in court-bouillon or baked in the oven in a sauce.

Garfish with Sauce Verte

675g (1½lb) filleted garfish
75g (3oz) softened butter
sea salt and freshly ground black
  pepper
300ml (½pt) single cream

3 tablespoons each of the
  following herbs, finely
  chopped: parsley, tarragon, dill
  or chervil

In a bowl mix all the herbs with the softened butter, adding the salt and the pepper. Take the garfish fillets and ensure that all the bones are removed. Spread each fillet with the softened herb butter and roll them up, place in a dish in a preheated oven at 375°F/190°C/Gas Mark 5 for 15–18 minutes. Take the dish from the oven and add the cream to the juices, reheat and baste the fish with the sauce. Serve at once.

Poached or baked garfish can be eaten with any of the herb butters (page 167) and some of the more strongly flavoured sauces (pages 170–74).

Grey Mullet

In season all the year round. They appear in shoals in the inshore waters around the south and west coasts of Britain. They have been condemned as having a muddy flavour. This is because they are herbivorous and extract vegetable food from the mud of estuaries and the inshore sea bed. I have come across this once when I caught the fish in the estuary of the Stour in Dorset. The muddy flavour was so strong that it was inedible. But I am told that this is rare and it has not occurred again. To be on the safe side, wash the fish repeatedly in running water and then soak it for 5 minutes in acidulated water (cold water with 1 tablespoon of vinegar or lemon juice added).

The fish is renowned and prized since ancient times for its roe, which was salted, pressed and preserved in barrels. Thin slivers of this roe were enjoyed as an appetizer in all the Eastern Mediterranean countries. Known as botargo, it was popular in England in the seventeenth and eighteenth centuries. Pepys mentions sitting up one night eating it while drinking. If it can be found now it is absurdly expensive, smoked cod's roe and the purée, taramasalata (see pages 116–17) have taken its place.

If you are lucky enough to buy a grey mullet which has its roe, extract it and use it separately (see roes, pages 33 and 50). Small mullets can be grilled or barbecued. Score the fish diagonally across and fill with a savoury butter. If the mullet weighs over 1.25kg (2½lb) stuff the fish and then bake it.

Baked Grey Mullet

1 grey mullet of 1.25kg (2½lb) or
  more
450g (1lb) tomatoes
2 onions
3 tablespoons olive oil

3 cloves garlic, crushed
1 teaspoon dried oregano
2 tablespoons tomato purée
sea salt and black pepper

For the stuffing

225g (8oz) mushrooms
50g (2oz) butter
50g (2oz) wholemeal
  breadcrumbs

1 egg yolk
sea salt and black pepper

Scale and clean the fish and put it aside. Chop the mushrooms small and cook them in the butter over quite a high flame so you are driving off the moisture (*á la duxelles*). When the mushrooms are cooked and dry pour them into a bowl and add the rest of the ingredients for the stuffing. Fill the cavities of the fish with this.

Peel and seed the tomatoes, chop the onions and add these to the oil in a pan with the garlic and dried oregano. Let them simmer for 15 minutes or until there is a thick sauce, add the tomato purée and the seasoning and cook for a further few minutes. Pour the sauce into a shallow baking pan large enough to contain the fish. Lay the stuffed fish on top of the sauce and protect the top of the fish with buttered paper. Place in a preheated oven at 350°F/180°C/Gas Mark 4 for 35 minutes, take the buttered paper away from the top of the fish for the last 10 minutes.

Use any of the recipes for stuffed, baked fish.
Fillets of mullet can be eaten with any of the herb butters or Parsley or Mornay Sauce (page 170).

Haddock

In season all the year round. One of the most popular fish in Britain second only to cod; used extensively in the fried fish and chip shops. One of the best smoked fish of them all (see pages 111 and 177). Lives in deep waters in the North Sea.

Small fish can be bought whole when they can be stuffed and baked. Larger fish are sold either as fillets or steaks. The flesh is white and firm and has excellent flavour. It can be plainly grilled and eaten with a strong sauce such as mustard or horseradish. It is excellent mixed with smoked haddock in fish pies.

Poached Haddock with Mustard Sauce

4 thick steaks of haddock	pinch of nutmeg
300ml (½pt) milk	sea salt and black pepper
2 bay leaves	

For the mustard sauce

50g (2oz) butter	2 tablespoons Dijon mustard
25g (1oz) flour	1 tablespoon Moutarde de Meaux
milk from the fish above	

Lay the haddock steaks in a shallow pan, pour over the milk and add the bay leaves, nutmeg, and seasoning. Place over a low flame and let the fish simmer gently for 5 minutes. Test that the steaks are done by inserting a knife between the bone and the flesh, if the flesh comes away easily they are cooked through, if not give them a few minutes more. Remove the steaks from the pan and cover them with buttered paper while you make the sauce. Discard the bay leaves from the liquor and reserve it for the sauce.

Melt the butter in a pan, add the flour and cook for a moment. Pour the milk and fish juices into the roux and cook until you have a smooth sauce, then stir in the mustards and continue to cook. Taste and check for seasoning. Pour the sauce onto a platter and place the steaks on top of it, garnish with lemon and parsley.

All of the cod recipes (pages 31–2) are suitable for haddock. Can also be used in fish soups and stews, see Chapter VII.
If plainly poached or baked, many of the herb butters and sauces in Chapter IX are suitable.

Hake

Available from November to August. Another fish that is popular in the fried fish and chip shops. The most common size is between 30 and 45cm (1 and 1½ft). The soft white flesh, like the cod and the haddock, needs the minimum of cooking. Hake can be bought whole or cut up into steaks; it can also be smoked or barbecued. The flesh tends to have less flavour than either cod or haddock, so it needs strong vigorous sauces or can be stuffed as in the recipe below.

Stuffed Hake

1 piece of hake weighing 1.25kg (2½lb)	25g (1oz) butter
	1 tablespoon chopped tarragon

For the stuffing

1 chopped onion	75g (3oz) wholemeal
2 tablespoons olive oil	breadcrumbs
50g (2oz) good blue cheese	1 tablespoon chopped parsley
1 tablespoon sage	1 teaspoon paprika
	sea salt and black pepper

Have the fishmonger skin and bone the fish but leave the head on. Liberally butter a large piece of foil, sprinkle half the tarragon on it and lay the fish on the foil. Now make the stuffing.

Cook the chopped onion in the olive oil until it is soft. Pour into a mixing bowl and add the rest of the ingredients, crumbling the cheese. Mix thoroughly. Stuff the fish with the mixture, smear more butter over the top of the fish and sprinkle with the rest of the tarragon. Twist the foil over so that the fish is completely enclosed and bake in a preheated oven at 350°F/180°C/ Gas Mark 4 for 35 minutes.

Steaks can be cooked as in:
Flétan au Poivre, page 48
Soft Herring Roes, page 50
Plaice with Coriander Butter, page 56
Skate with Capers, page 62
Giant Prawns with Garlic, page 134
Gratin of Scampi and Avocado, page 105
Poached Scallops in White Wine, page 103
Large pieces of hake can be cooked as in:
Red Mullet in Vine Leaves, page 135
Swordfish with Croutons, page 139
Casserole of Tuna, page 141
Stewed Octopus with Garlic and Tomato Sauce, page 133
If plainly grilled or poached, many of the herb butters, mayonnaises and sauces in Chapter IX are suitable.

Halibut

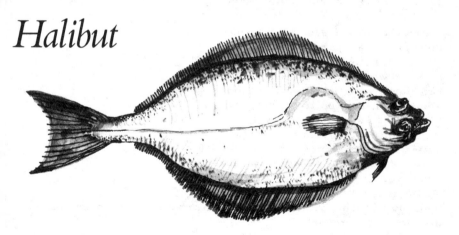

In season all the year round. The largest of the flat fish, halibut can grow as long as 2½m (8ft) and weigh 300kg (660lb). There was a fish 60 years old, caught at Grimsby in 1959 that weighed 252kg (504lb). It lives in the cold deep waters of the North Sea and because it grows slowly, it is one of the fish which is not caught as often as they were. This is why it is expensive. It is bought as steaks, but avoid the tail end which can be dry. However a little of this fish goes a long way as it is highly nutritious, full of vitamin D. It should be treated with great care and the best method of cooking the steaks is to lightly poach them in a strong fumet, or to grill them with plenty of herb butter, but take care that they do not dry out. If the steaks are poached they are very good cold with a herb mayonnaise. Another excellent way of cooking the fish is to treat it like meat and fry them *au poivre*.

Flétan au Poivre

4 thick steaks of halibut
3 tablespoons black peppercorns
1 tablespoon flour
1 teaspoon sea salt
100g (4oz) butter

2 tablespoons olive oil
50ml (2fl oz) brandy
50ml (2 fl oz) port
150ml (¼pt) chicken stock
150ml (¼pt) double cream

Crush the peppercorns with a mortar and pestle, add them to the flour and the salt, rub this into the steaks. Melt half of the butter with the oil in a frying pan and cook the fish gently, for about 10 minutes. Flame with the brandy, deglaze the pan with the port then pour in the stock. Remove the fish to a hot serving platter and bring the sauce to the boil, stir in the cream and the rest of the butter. Check for seasoning before pouring over the fish.

Can also be used in the following recipes:
Lotte Provençale, page 26
Roulade de Lotte, page 26
Roast Eel with Apples and Cider, pages 36–7
Fish Simmered in Ginger and Soy Sauce, page 39
Roes with Green Peppercorns and Cream, page 50
Dory in Cider and Cream, pages 51–2
Plaice with Coriander Butter, page 56
Skate with Capers, page 62
Gratin of Scampi and Avocado, page 105
Fish Salad, pages 121–2
Soufflé, page 123
If plainly grilled or poached, many of the herb butters, mayonnaises and sauces in Chapter IX are suitable.

Herring

In season from April to November. Herrings are now reappearing in the shops as a ban on herring fishing was lifted in 1984. But sadly we seem to have forgotten how to cook them. They are probably the cheapest and most highly nutritious food available to us. They are as high in protein as lean beef and rich in the A, B and D vitamins. Because large numbers of them are split and smoked to become kippers the roes are sold separately. Both the soft and the hard roes are delicious and make a separate dish (see below). Herrings are also salted and pickled and are a great delicacy in the Scandinavian countries (see page 112). Soused herring is a Scottish recipe as is the one below. Herrings, like mackerel and sprats, are rich in oil; if grilled do not add any more fat, but it is best to score the fish diagonally across with three gashes on each side so that they are cooked evenly through. A preference of mine is to fill these gashes with chopped garlic, it cuts across the oiliness of the fish and is a practice I learned on the Dalmatian coast of Yugoslavia.

Scottish Herrings

4 herrings   sea salt and black pepper
75g (3oz) coarse oatmeal   75g (3oz) smoked bacon fat★

Clean and gut the herrings. Mix the oatmeal with plenty of sea salt and black pepper, coat the herrings with the mixture. Melt the bacon fat in a pan and fry the herrings until they are crisp and brown. Serve with lemon wedges and garnish with parsley.

Gingered Soused Herring

6 herrings   pinch each of ground cumin and
sea salt and freshly ground black   coriander
  pepper   3 bay leaves
25g (1oz) ginger root sliced   150ml (5fl oz) water
1 large onion, sliced   150ml (5fl oz) red wine vinegar

★If you do not wish to use bacon, because of the unnatural brutality of the dry sow stalls where two thirds of our pigs are now reared, use a mixture of butter and olive oil.

Cut the heads from the herrings, clean and trim the fish and split them down the middle. Discard the backbone and sprinkle with salt and pepper. Cut them in half and roll each half up neatly. Place in a baking dish and insert the pieces of ginger root among them with the onion, spices and bay leaves. Pour over the water and red wine vinegar and bake in a preheated oven at 275°F/140°C/ Gas Mark 1 for 1½ hours. Serve cold.

Herring Roes

Soft herring roes can be bought separately in the fishmongers by weight. They are cheap and highly nutritious. Soft herring roes are also canned and in this state they are far more expensive. Herring roes can also be bought frozen. Freezing does not affect their flavour but does make them more difficult to handle. They are very soft and can easily go into a tacky paste. Herring roes need to be lightly floured then fried in butter. They are done when just crisp and light brown. Fresh herbs may be added, or spices as in the recipe below.

Roes with Green Peppercorns and Cream

225g (8oz) soft herring roes
flour for coating
25g (1oz) butter
150ml (5fl oz) dry white wine

zest and juice of 1 lemon
½ teaspoon sea salt
1 tablespoon green peppercorns
150ml (5fl oz) single cream

Lightly flour the herring roes and melt the butter in a shallow pan. Fry the roes briefly so that they are just beginning to cook, then add the white wine, zest and juice of lemon, salt, and green peppercorns. Cook for two minutes more so that the wine reduces by half, then add the cream and stir to make a sauce.

Herrings can be cooked simply, floured and fried as sprat and smelt or plainly baked in the oven. All sauces that go with mackerel will also do with the herring: Mustard (page 171), Caper (page 173), Green Peppercorn (page 173), Spiced (page 173), Hot Pepper (page 174), Horseradish (page 174) and Hot Tomato (page 174).

John Dory

A fairly uncommon fish though specialist fishmongers in the south and west of England are beginning to stock it. In season all the year round. It is about 30–40cm (12–16 inches) long but can grow to double that length. It appears to be mostly head, which is a fearsome sight, but the head itself is indispensible for fish soups and stocks. Steaks can be cut from the body, which is less than half of the fish. Remove the thick skin before cooking. Dory can often be eaten in Venice where it is generally served cold with mayonnaise. This is not always the perfect treatment. Far more delicious is the Devon recipe below.

Dory in Cider and Cream

4 steaks of dory, about 2.5cm (1 inch) thick
3 tablespoons flour
50g (2oz) butter
1 tablespoon olive oil
1 tablespoon lemon juice

1 tablespoon each of parsley, fennel, tarragon, basil
150ml (5fl oz) dry cider
sea salt and black pepper
2 tablespoons double cream

Skin the steaks and roll them in the flour. Heat the butter and oil in a pan and fry the steaks until they are brown. Add the herbs, lemon juice and cider and continue to cook for a few minutes. Take the steaks out of the pan and lay them on a platter. Season the sauce in the pan and then add the cream, cook for another minute until you have a smooth sauce then pour it over the fish.

Can also be substituted in:
Lotte Provençale, page 26
Roast Eels with Apples and Cider, pages 36–7
Fish Simmered in Ginger and Soy Sauce, page 39
Flounder à la Deauvillaise, pages 41–2
Flétan au Poivre, page 48
Plaice with Coriander Butter, page 56
Turbot with Crab Sauce, page 66
French method with Whiting, page 68
Giant Prawns with Garlic, page 134
Poached Scallops in White Wine, page 103
Creamed Prawns and Rice, page 101
Gratin of Scampi and Avocado, page 105
Soufflé, page 123
If plainly grilled or poached, many of the herb butters, mayonnaises and sauces in Chapter IX are suitable.

Lemon Sole

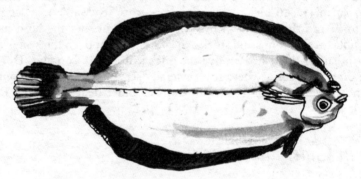

In season all the year round and widely available. Another flat fish which has less flavour than Dover sole, it too can be filleted and all the recipes for sole will be suitable. However giving lemon sole the *haute cuisine* treatment seems a waste of time. It is a fish which needs simple cooking. It makes excellent fish cakes and is a good ingredient for fish pies, or try frying or grilling with butter. Sole Meunière which is usually done with Dover sole works well for the more modest lemon sole.

Sole Meunière

4 fillets of lemon sole
seasoned flour
75g (3oz) butter*

juice and zest of 1 lemon
parsley and quartered lemon to
garnish

Make sure the fishmonger has skinned the fillets. Roll them in the seasoned flour. Melt half of the butter in a pan and fry the fillets, turning them carefully so that they don't break. Continue to cook until they are golden brown – about 5–6 minutes. Take the fish out of the pan and lay it on a platter. Put the rest of the butter into the pan with the zest and lemon juice. Melt and mix it together and pour over the fish. Garnish with sprigs of parsley and the lemon quarters.

Mackerel

Widely available and in season between December and July. Like the herring the mackerel is highly nutritious in its vitamins and minerals. It is still very cheap to buy. The fish is usually about 30cm (12 inches) long, bright silver with a striped blue and black back. It is a distant cousin of that tasty leviathan of the sea the tunny fish. The flesh of the mackerel is very rich so a little goes a long way. It smokes well and will make an excellent pâté (see pages

*If you are concerned about saturated fat intake, omit butter and use olive oil, but this cannot then be called 'meunière'. Here, I would add half a teaspoon of asafoetida to the oil, or one clove of crushed garlic.

159–60). It can be filleted and soused like herring (see pages 49–50) or pickled in white wine.

But it must be eaten fresh; because of its oiliness it will go off quickly and the pong of a tired fish is not attractive. Mackerel needs an astringent sauce to cut through its richness. The classic is one made from gooseberries, but sorrel, rhubarb, cranberry, redcurrant or mustard will do very nicely. The fish can be barbecued or baked in the oven with or without foil, but the simplest method is to grill the fish and serve it with the sauce. Always score the fish deeply, diagonally across before grilling.

Grilled Mackerel with Gooseberry Sauce

4 mackerel   sea salt and black pepper
butter for basting

For the sauce
450g (1lb) gooseberries   1 red chilli or dash Tabasco

Score the fish diagonally across, three times on each side. Rub sea salt and freshly ground black pepper into the flesh then place on some buttered foil beneath a medium grill. Place a little more butter on top of the fish while it is cooking. Top and tail the gooseberries and put them in a pan without any water but with the chilli or the Tabasco. Place the pan over a low heat with the lid on and let the fruit cook in its own juice, about 5–8 minutes. When the fruit is cooked take out the chillis and put it through a sieve, keep the resulting purée warm. Turn the fish over and let them cook thoroughly on both sides. Serve the fish on a platter with the sauce separately.

See herring (page 50) for all the sauces to be used with mackerel. Also can be soused.

Pilchard

They are still caught off the coast of south-west England in the summer months. They are in season from April to November. They are another nutritious fish, part of the herring family, high in oil content and thus will deteriorate quickly. Most of the catch is used for canning. There is confusion between the pilchard and the sardine. They are the same fish. The pilchard is an adult sardine. But in the United States and in Europe there is a tendency to call all small fish which are canned 'sardines'.

If you find any fresh pilchards buy them and cook them like herrings. Grill or roll them in oatmeal and fry. But they are best barbecued immediately after they are caught. As most of us never see fresh pilchard and are stuck with the tins in the store cupboard, here is a quick supper dish, which improves them no end.

Pilchards Tossed in Whisky★

1 large tin of pilchards, canned in oil
150ml (5fl oz) whisky

black pepper
4 slices wholemeal toast
butter

Drain the oil from the pilchards and place the fish in a pan with the whisky. Raise the heat and toss the fish round to cover each piece without breaking it. The whisky should be almost burnt away. Give the fish some good hefty grinds of the pepper mill. Have the toast ready, butter it liberally and place a portion of pilchards and some of its juice on each piece.

★This recipe came from Bush, the butler to the writer Julian Fane, who would enquire of guests after the theatre, 'Would Sir like sardines tossed in whisky?' Sir always did.

Plaice

Widely available and in season all the year round. One of the most familiar of British fish, certainly the most famous. Its flavour can be ruined by freezing and institutional overcooking.

It can be 50cm (20 inches) long, sometimes more. But most plaice we buy are 30cm (12 inches) or less. They can be grilled, fried or gently poached whole. They can also be filleted and any of the flatfish recipes will be suitable.

Scandinavia and the Netherlands eat far more plaice per head of population than we do, so here is a Dutch recipe.

Plaice with Coriander Butter

allow 1 plaice per person
100g (4oz) butter
juice and zest of 1 lemon
1 tablespoon coriander seeds,
   finely crushed

1 tablespoon chopped dill weed
1 tablespoon chopped tarragon
sea salt and black pepper

Lay the fish in a shallow pan and just cover with salted water. Bring the water to the boil and simmer for 5 minutes. Turn the heat off, cover the pan and then make the sauce. Melt the butter, add the lemon juice and zest, then all the other ingredients. Cook for a moment until the butter is frothing then drain the fish carefully, place on a platter and pour the sauce over it.

Can also be substituted in any of the flat fish recipes. Is also good in fish soups, stews and pies (see Chapter VII) and fish cakes (page 57).
Many of the herb butters, mayonnaises and sauces in Chapter IX are suitable.

Pollack

A member of the cod family available all the year round which thrives in British coastal waters. It is often confused with coley and when filleted is often sold in the fishmongers under that name. To confuse matters more, coley is called pollock in the USA. They can reach 1 metre (39 inches) in length and they live off sand eels and small fish on the sea bottom in coastal waters. The flesh can be dry but it is of good flavour, any of the cod or haddock recipes are suitable.

Fish Cakes

450g (1lb) pollack, coley, whiting, cod, haddock or hake
450g (1lb) potatoes
50g (2oz) butter
25g (1oz) plain flour
150ml (5fl oz) milk
1 tsp. powdered mustard
1 tsp. Worcestershire sauce
pinch of cayenne, coriander and cumin
sea salt and black pepper
generous handful of chopped parsley
toasted wholemeal breadcrumbs
oil for frying

Steam the fish over the boiling potatoes, let it cool and discard all the skin and bones. Mash the potatoes well with half of the butter. Make a roux with the rest of the butter and the flour. Add the milk and make a thick sauce. Mix the fish and potato together and add the sauce and all the flavourings, and chopped parsley. Refrigerate for an hour. Fashion into cakes and roll in the breadcrumbs; fry in the oil until crisp and brown.

Can be substituted in any of the cod (pages 31–2) or haddock (pages 45–6) recipes. Is an excellent fish for soups, pies and stews. (See Chapter VII).

Red Mullet

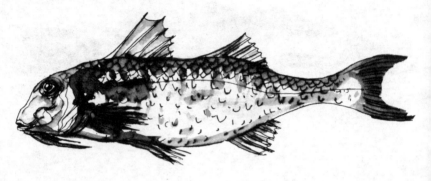

This was a hugely popular fish with the Romans and appears on many mosaic floors. It was also popular in Victorian England. It lives mostly in the Mediterranean, but migrates to the waters of Southern Britain in the summer months. Available now in more and more fishmongers, in season from June to August.

They are never gutted and are nicknamed the woodcock of the sea, because of the slight gut flavour which permeates the flesh. They can be fried, grilled or barbecued. I find them rather bony and thus annoying, but I enjoy them most, freshly caught and barbecued over herb twigs, rosemary or fennel.

Red Mullet with Fennel

allow 1 red mullet to each person   2 tablespoons fennel seeds
seasoned flour   50–75g (2–3oz) butter

For the sauce

2 fennel bulbs   sea salt and black pepper
75ml (2fl oz) anise or Pernod   2 tablespoons double cream

Cover the fish in seasoned flour. Crush the fennel seeds and melt the butter in a large pan. Cook the fennel seeds in the butter for a moment before adding the fish. Fry the mullet over a medium flame, turning them once so that they are crisp and brown. Meanwhile make the sauce: chop the fennel bulbs and put them in a little salted water until soft, about 10 minutes. Drain them then liquidize and put through a sieve. Return the purée to a pan, add the anise or Pernod and taste for seasoning. Beat in the cream when the purée is warm and bring it gradually back to the heat but do not boil. Place the fish on a platter and serve the sauce separately.

Shad

Part of the herring family, there are several varieties. The Allis shad is the most common and makes a popular dish in the Gironde. If caught in the sea the flesh is often thin and dry, but once the fish have entered the river during the spring to spawn they become plump and the flesh has a delicate flavour. The main problem with shad are the bones which are difficult to extract from the flesh, but long slow cooking renders them soft and edible. The best policy is to get a friendly Girondais to teach you how to extract the bones and then to show you how *alose à l'oseille* is cooked.

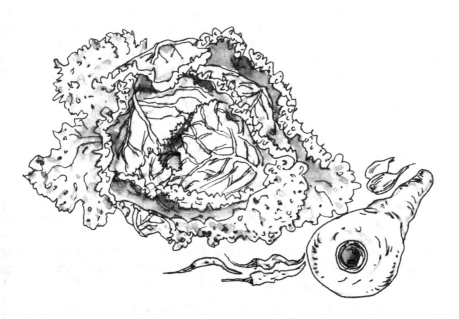

Shark

A superlative fish – read on.

This is the porbeagle shark which grows to around 3 metres and weighs about 200kg. It often hunts herring and mackerel and can damage fishing nets by raiding them. The fish swims in the North Atlantic around the coast of Britain, in the English Channel, on the coasts of Europe from Norway down to Spain, and in the Mediterranean, as well as across the Atlantic to Newfoundland. It is the enterprising and active Norwegian fishing fleet which catches it, freezes the flesh and exports it to Germany where in turn it is exported to us. The French, who of course know a thing or two about an excellent fish, refer to it as *veau de mer* and, for a non-meat-eater, this is where my own palate revels in a vicarious pleasure.

I mention this because lately I have discovered the frozen steaks on sale in fishmongers here, and freezing the flesh appears to do no harm at all. Guests who have eaten the shark ask me with rising suspicion, 'Is this pork or chicken?' On being told the truth, they are still enthusiastic. It was not always so; both in the UK and in the US, this fish was disdained and there are barely disguised superior references to it being eaten only in the Mediterranean, as if those palates knew no better. I suspect the reason was an atavistic one and that the thought of shark meant, in people's minds, a man-eating fish – hence, cannibalism. To me, this idea of recycling food is rather appealing. However, it cannot be entertained, for the porbeagle, though a voracious eater of fish, is considered harmless to man.★

The shark steaks can be treated like swordfish, plainly grilled with butter and lemon. Or baked *en papillote* or *en croûte*. My own favourite recipe, which owes its inspiration to the Far East, is opposite.

★A nineteenth-century writer swears a fish sprang out of the water and tore the clothes off a fisherman. This sounds like a tall story to me, for a fish that size would surely have dragged the man back into the sea.

Indonesian Casserole of Vegetables and Shark

4 large steaks of shark (thawed)
seasoned flour
3 tablespoons olive oil
1 tsp. each mustard seeds,
    turmeric, fenugreek and cumin
50g (2oz) ginger root, peeled and
    finely sliced

3 cloves of garlic, finely sliced
2 onions, finely sliced
2 green peppers, cored, seeded
    and sliced
675g (1½lb) new potatoes, sliced
225g (8oz) mushrooms, sliced

Cut away the black skin from the steaks and cut the flesh into 5cm (2inch) square pieces. Turn them in seasoned flour. Heat the oil in a large casserole and throw in the spices. Let them fry for a moment, then add the pieces of fish. Turn the fish in the oil and spices and then add 1.25 litres (2 pints) of water and all the vegetables. Bring to the boil and simmer on top of the stove for 50 to 60 minutes. Give a good stir and check for seasoning.
    Serve with boiled rice.

Shark steaks can also be substituted in the following recipes:
Lotte Provençale, page 26
Roulade de Lotte, page 26
Marmite, page 31
Roast Eel with Apples and Cider, pages 36–7
Flounder à la Deauvillaise, pages 41–2
Roes with Green Peppercorns and Cream, page 50
Dory in Cider and Cream, pages 51–2
Turbot with Crab Sauce, page 66
Truite-saumonée en Croûte, page 82
Creamed Prawns with Rice, page 101
Poached Scallops in White Wine, page 103
Gratin of Scampi and Avocado, page 105
Soufflé, page 123
Kedgeree, pages 118–9
If plainly poached, many of the herb butters, mayonnaises and sauces in
Chapter IX are suitable.

Skate

Widely available and in season throughout the winter months from August to April. One of the best fish to be found in British waters and a particular favourite of mine. Only the wings are on the fishmongers slab and their tough black skin has been torn off using pliers. A strenuous and difficult task, even for an experienced fisherman. The whole fish can be 90cm (3 feet) in length and almost as broad. All the skate are members of the shark family and so have cartilaginous bones.

It is an easy fish to cook and consume for the flesh peels off the soft wing bones with ease. The fish can be grilled, barbecued or fried. It can also be eaten cold in a mixed fish salad and goes well with crab. As the flesh jellies it is excellent for mousses, terrines and pâtés. The classic recipes are with black butter and capers and I give one below.

Skate with Capers

allow 1 wing of skate per person
seasoned flour
100g (4oz) butter

3 tablespoons capers
2 tablespoons red wine vinegar

Flour both sides of the skate and melt half the butter in a large pan. Fry the skate on both sides and keep the pieces warm in the oven. When they are all cooked, melt the remaining butter in the pan and add the capers; deglaze the pan by pouring in the vinegar and stirring until you have a bubbling dark brown sauce. Pour this over the skate and serve.

Can also be substituted in:
Roast Eels with Apple and Cider, pages 36–7
Flounder à la Deauvillaise, pages 41–2
Flétan au Poivre, page 48
Roes with Green Peppercorns and Cream, page 50
Dory in Cider and Cream, pages 51–2
Plaice with Coriander Butter, page 56
Devilled like whitebait, page 67
Soufflé, page 123
Excellent cold in fish salads and good with crab, scallops, scampi and shrimps.
If plainly cooked, many of the herb butters, mayonnaises and sauces in Chapter IX are suitable.

Smelt

These are cousins of the salmon and are found as far south as Turkey and as far north as Oslo. They swim up rivers to spawn but stay within the brackish waters. They are a precious delicacy in France but in Britain they are only used to feed cattle. This illustrates perfectly our different national characteristics in the way we treat food.

Smelt smell deliciously of cucumber, some even divine a whiff of violet. Like all fish they are best cooked as soon after they are caught as is possible, when they are generally fried. Gut and scale them, roll them in seasoned flour then fry them in butter and oil.

Sprat

Widely available and in season through the winter months. Part of the herring family and a popular fish in Scandinavia and the Baltic States. In Norway they net shoals of these fish in the fjords and can them in oil, when they are sold as brisling.

They are small, usually about 10cm (4 inches) long and should be floured and fried in oil. They make excellent eating and like the other members of this family are high in nutrition. There is no need to gut them; fry them whole, you can avoid the head and backbone easily by dissecting them on the plate, though if the fish are larger than above I tend to behead them before cooking.

They have one major drawback: while they are cooking, they have a pernicious pong that fills the house and remains for some hours. Because of this, my mother-in-law refused to cook sprats for her husband, who adored them, more than once a year.

They can be smoked and also barbecued by stabbing eight or ten through the head with a long skewer and laying them over the fire for a few minutes. Eat them with plenty of lemon and black pepper.

Filets de Sole Véronique, page 40.

Baked Grey Mullet, page 44.

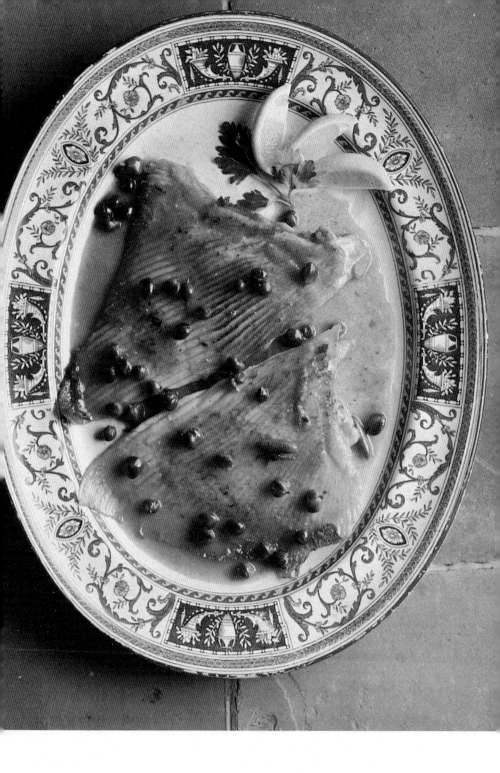

Skate with Capers, page 62.

Salmon in Spinach Parcels, page 80.

Cold Lobster with Spencer's Sauce, page 95.

Mussels with Herb Butter, page 97.

Globe Artichokes Stuffed with Prawns, page 101.

Poached Scallops in White Wine, page 103.

Sturgeon

The common sturgeon is found very occasionally in British coastal waters. He is not to be confused with the beluga sturgeon which lives in the Caspian and Black Seas and whose roe is eaten as caviar. He is, however, part of the same family. They are one of the most ancient fish, unique in that they have a skeleton composed of both cartilage and bone. They are rarely caught now as there is a fear that the species may be diminishing. In the past they often formed part of a course in a banquet and were roasted like great hunks of meat.

Caviar importers and distributors also deal to a lesser degree with the fish itself and they smoke the fish like salmon. It is a great delicacy (and very expensive), and is eaten with lemon, cayenne pepper, brown bread and butter.

Turbot

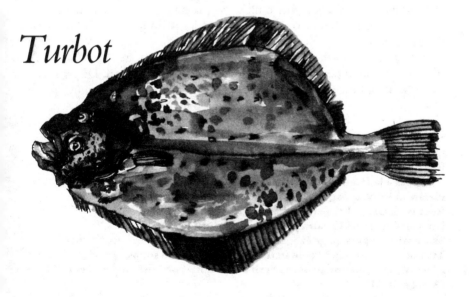

In season all the year round, but because most turbot goes to the catering trade only a few of the smaller fish are available in the shops.

One of the great flat fish renowned in cuisine and inspiring many recipes. It is a huge treat to find a handsome turbot. Diamond shaped fish kettles, called *turbotières*, can be bought in which to poach the large fish.

If the fish is not too large it can be grilled and fried in butter. If it will not fit into a pan or under the grill it can be wrapped in foil with herbs and butter and baked in the oven. The fish can also be filleted and then all the recipes for sole are suitable.

The best way, it seems to me, is to poach the fish and use the liquid to make a sauce as in the recipe below.

Turbot with Crab Sauce

1 turbot weighing about 1kg (2¼lb)	2 bay leaves
300ml (½pt) milk	sea salt and black pepper
	25g (1oz) butter

For the sauce

flesh from 1 crab	bunch parsley, finely chopped
3 tablespoons double cream	milk in which the fish has cooked

If there is no fish kettle or frying pan big enough for the fish, use a baking tray. Lay the fish in it and pour the milk over, place the bay leaves in the milk and season it. Dot the butter over the fish and let it simmer gently for 15 to 20 minutes. Meanwhile make the sauce.

In a bowl mix the cream, crab meat and parsley together. When the fish is cooked through pour the liquid from the fish into the bowl. Discard the bay leaves and pour the sauce into a pan, heating gently but not allowing it to boil. Place the fish on a platter and pour the sauce over it.

Steaks of turbot can be cooked as in:
Lotte Provençale, page 26
Roast Eels with Apples and Cider, pages 36–7
Flounder à la Deauvillaise, pages 41–2
Flétan au Poivre, page 48
Roes with Green Peppercorns and Cream, page 50
Dory in Cider and Cream, pages 51–2
Skate with Capers, page 62
Turbot is also excellent cold in mixed fish salads and soups.
If plainly cooked, many of the herb butters, mayonnaises and sauces in Chapter IX are suitable.

Whitebait

These are thought to be a species of very small fish, but are in fact a mixture of the fry of herrings and sprats and diverse others. There have been up to twenty different species in some catches that are called whitebait. They are now difficult to obtain fresh, but their season is between January and September. They were hugely popular in the nineteenth century, when whitebait dinners were given beside the Thames.

Now they tend to reach supermarkets frozen in a bag. These are perfectly edible if not quite as good as eating them fresh.

There is only one way of dealing with them. Dust them in seasoned flour and fry them in oil. Eat them with masses of lemon and they can be extra good if covered in chopped parsley. For devilled whitebait, add cayenne pepper to the seasoned flour. The job of frying them is much helped if you have a deep fryer and a chip basket. But I find a wok can be a useful deep fryer and you don't then have to use large quantities of oil.

Whiting

Widely available and in season all the year round. Part of the cod family and famed as invalid food because of its delicacy: that generally means lack of flavour, so is off-putting for all of us who are not invalids. The French value the fish highly and have many recipes for *merlans*; this should tell us that the fish is worthy of the finest cooking.

They can be grilled or fried – the fishmonger will fillet or bone the fish. They can also be baked in foil or without, smoked or barbecued over herb twigs. Like cod they will take strong sauces. The French cook them with mussels and mushrooms, with onions, cider and gruyère, with olives and in white wine. But the recipe below is adapted from Scotland where they also value this fish.

Whiting in Herb Sauce

4 whiting
seasoned flour
75g (3oz) butter
3 tablespoons milk
sea salt and black pepper

150ml (¼pt) single cream
3 tablespoons of each of the
    following herbs, finely
    chopped: parsley, tarragon,
    chives and basil

Roll the cleaned fish in the seasoned flour. Melt the butter in a pan and fry them on one side. Turn them over and let them begin to cook on the other side. Mix the rest of the ingredients together and pour over the fish. Continue to cook for 3–4 minutes, basting them in the sauce. Serve them in a dish in the sauce.

Can be substituted for any of the cod (pages 31–2) or haddock (pages 45–6) recipes.
If plainly cooked, many of the herb butters, mayonnaises and sauces (Chapter IX) are suitable.

CHAPTER III

FRESHWATER FISH

'The charm of fishing is that it is the pursuit of what is elusive but attainable, a perpetual series of occasions for hope.'

John Buchan

Bream

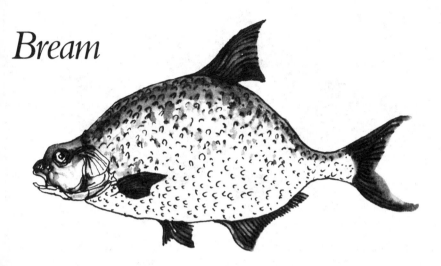

Found all over Europe and England in lakes and slow flowing rivers. Usually between 30 and 50cm (12 and 20 inches) in size it can grow up to 80cm (32 inches). Must be scaled with care, for the fish has loose, large scales which, though they come off easily, are sharp if missed. Can be filleted but is more usually cooked whole, baked in foil or barbecued. A firm white flesh of great delicacy. Follow recipes for any large stuffed baked fish, or this routine for a barbecued one.

Barbecued Fish

Mix equal parts of lemon juice and olive oil together and crush a couple of garlic cloves into it. Season liberally with salt and black pepper and paint the whole fish with the oil and lemon. Lay the fish in a shallow dish and let the oil and lemon run down the sides; continue to baste it for an hour before it is cooked.

Meanwhile have the charcoal at the glowing red stage and lay over the grill, if possible, either some fennel twigs or rosemary. Lay the fish on these, secured in a wire clamp if you have one. Allow five minutes cooking to each side and roll the fish over with the help of implements and friends. The fennel or rosemary helps in moving the fish around.

Carp

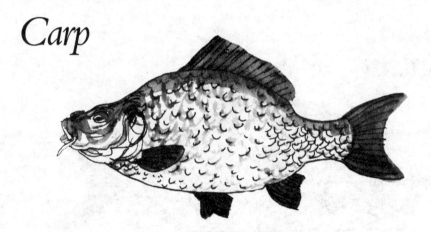

Carp live in streams and ponds, are herbivorous, so like the grey mullet can taste muddy.* They are caught by anglers but also farmed. They appear in specialist fishmongers and can be ordered from them, available all the year round, but they are seen in the shops in the festive season, from November to January. They are a popular fish in France, Germany and China.

They can live sometimes for forty years and will grow to enormous size. To counteract the possible muddy taste, soak in acidulated water for up to 5 minutes then rinse under the cold tap. The farmed carp will be around 1.5kg (3lb) in weight, its flesh should be firm and sweet. The Germans eat it on Christmas Eve with a powerful horseradish sauce and, like the Chinese, with a sweet-and-sour sauce. It is often cooked in wine, with sorrel, with fruits and, as below, with chestnuts. It can be grilled, fried, poached or baked, in foil or without.

I have not tried it, but I suspect its sweet flavour would be destroyed by smoking, and barbecueing might also be too tough a treatment.

---

*Dorothy Hartley in *Food in England* tells how she was taught by an old Fens' fisherman how to cook pond fish so that it will not taste muddy. Move the fish gently (the reason will become obvious), do not scale or wash or gut it, but cover it with a clay or flour-and-water paste completely. Then bake the fish, keeping it flat and without turning the fish. When the fish is done, break off the crust and the skin and scales will come off with it. The flesh, she says, will be clean tasting and of very fine quality.

The scales of pond fish are overlapping and fringe scales, which keep the mud clear from the fish's skin while the fish swims against the stream, but in still waters, the fish is limp and the scales open, so that the mud gets under them and touches the absorbent skin of the fish.

The theory is that moving the fish, even after it is dead, disturbs the mud so that it might flow or ooze into the flesh more, but the flour-and-water paste draws out the mud like a sponge.

I have not tried out this theory but it appeals to me.

Stuffed Carp with Chestnut Sauce

1 carp weighing about 1.5kg (3lb)   50g (2oz) butter

For the stuffing

75g (3oz) dried chestnuts   25g (1oz) butter
2 hard-boiled eggs   1 beaten egg
1 tablespoon sage   sea salt and black pepper
2 tablespoons wholemeal
   breadcrumbs

For the sauce

75g (3oz) chestnut purée   2 tablespoons double cream
150ml (¼pt) dry white wine   sea salt and black pepper

Soak the dried chestnuts overnight then put them, with the water they have
soaked in, in a pan. Bring to the boil and let them simmer for an hour. When
they are cool chop them up roughly with the chopped hard-boiled eggs, sage
and breadcrumbs, mix in the butter and the beaten egg and season to taste.
Clean and prepare the fish then stuff it with the mixture. Butter a large piece of
foil copiously and lay the fish on it, dot with more butter and fold the foil over
the fish making a complete parcel. Bake in a preheated oven at 400°F/200°C/
Gas Mark 6 for 30 minutes. Meanwhile make the sauce by beating together all
the ingredients in a saucepan over a gentle heat. Serve the sauce separately
from the fish. Unfold the foil parcel and gently remove the fish to a platter,
pouring the juices over it. Serve with lemon wedges and garnish with parsley.

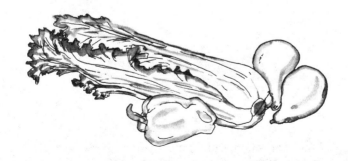

Char

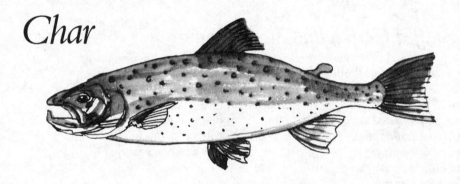

A member of the salmon family still found in lakes in England, Scotland and Ireland. Not available in the shops but it is in season in the summer months. It can be grilled, poached or baked in the oven with or without foil. The recipes for trout or salmon are all suitable. It would, I imagine, smoke as well as its cousins. In the Lake District they used to sell pots of buttered char (see fish pastes pages 159–60).

Eels

In season all the year round, caught mostly by anglers. Not widely available, but sometimes found in fishmongers or in specialist Eel Shops as in the East End of London. There you can buy your eels live as well as jellied.

When I was a small child my father often took me eel fishing. Sometimes we would return at the end of the day with fifteen or twenty of these black, slimy river snakes. My father dealt with the problem of chopping them up as no one else in the family could stand the gore and the fact that the eels appeared to be still alive. Bits of eel would jump about the kitchen table, and even when they were floured and frying, contrive to twitch in the pan. Most of these eels would be poached in a large saucepan with pickling spices. They would be left to jelly overnight and then potted and kept in the larder.

Eels should be fat and black, if brown they are still too young. They smoke beautifully and that is when I enjoy them most, though they are excellent in a pie served cold for a summer picnic.

Eel Pie

2 or 3 eels weighing 500g (1¼lb)
seasoned flour
225g (8oz) onions
½ tsp. mace
½ tsp. ground coriander
3 tablespoons chopped tarragon

½ bottle dry white wine
50g (2oz) butter
sea salt and black pepper
175g (6oz) wholemeal shortcrust
  pastry

Skin and bone the eels then chop them into 2.5cm (1 inch) pieces, discarding the head and tail. Roll each piece in seasoned flour. Chop up the onion coarsely and choosing a large pie dish fill it with the eel and onion as closely packed as possible. Sprinkle over the spices and the tarragon, pour in the wine and dot with the butter. Roll out the pastry and fit the top to the pie. Preheat the oven to 350°F/180°C/Gas Mark 4 and bake for 45 minutes protecting the pastry for the first half hour with buttered paper. Let the pie cool; it's best to leave it for a day when it will have jellied nicely.

Elvers

Elvers are three-year-old eels which can be seen in huge numbers as they swim up river in the spring. They occur all over Europe and are caught in nets and kept in buckets from which they are sometimes sold in markets. Many of the elvers are sent to eel farms in northern Europe. The elvers which survive their journey up river will take a further eight years to reach sexual maturity when they turn silver and start their journey back to the breeding grounds in the Sargasso Sea.

To remove the slime from the elvers, soak them in salt water, changing the water several times. Drain them well, shake them in a bag with flour and fry them like whitebait in bacon fat or hot olive oil.

Grayling

This fish lives in swiftly flowing streams and cold lakes throughout northern Europe, Russia and some parts of eastern Europe. They look and taste a little like trout, but they have a very large dorsal fin. They are a sport fish in Britain where they may be caught like trout with flies. If found, they are well worth eating and any trout recipe is suitable. Sensibly, the Russians have farmed them.

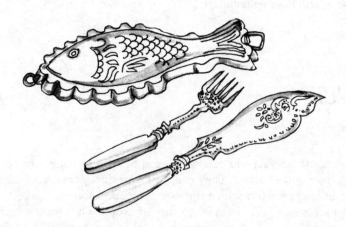

Perch

In season all the year round but only caught by anglers. One of the great fresh water fish honoured in ancient Greece and Rome, still eaten with great pleasure in Italy where more recipes exist than in France. China reveres the fish as well and perhaps your best opportunity of tasting it is to choose perch at a reliable Chinese restaurant.

If you are lucky enough to acquire a fresh one it should be scaled immediately after being caught; the spines can be painful so wear gloves. Plunge it first into boiling water with vinegar and leave for a few seconds, then it will descale easily.

Grill, fry or poach the fish, use a strong fish fumet for poaching, then skin the fish and serve with any of the sauces on pages 170–74.

Sauces suitable for perch are Crab (page 170), Anchovy (page 170), Mussel (page 170), Herb (page 171), Fennel (page 171), Crab and Brandy (page 172), Hollandaise (page 172), Tarragon (page 174). All of the herb butters and mayonnaises in Chapter IX would also go well.

Pike

This is a large handsome fish caught by anglers. In Britain you never see pike in the shops. It is in season from August to February. It lives in lakes and rivers and is a predator on everything else in its habitat including other pike. It was a favourite fish of Isaac Walton, the seventeenth-century author of *The Compleat Angler*, who gives a famous recipe, where the fish is stuffed with oysters, anchovies, spices, herbs and a pound of butter.

Pike has a unique flavour but it does tend to be dry which is why it is used for quenelles (see page 93). It also has one major drawback for me, the white meaty flesh can abound with tiny soft bones which are annoying. These bones are a positive help for making the quenelles for they are pounded into a purée and help to stiffen the dumplings.

My father was always very proud when he caught a pike, feeling that he had won a battle. We used to eat it stuffed and baked in the oven. This is the stuffing that my mother used to make.

Baked Stuffed Pike

1 pike weighing 1.5kg (3lb) or more	50g (2oz) butter

For the stuffing

25g (8oz) mushrooms, sliced	1 tsp. garam masala
1 onion, finely chopped	dash of tabasco
25g (1oz) butter	50g (2oz) wholemeal
1 beaten egg	breadcrumbs
1 tablespoon fresh thyme	sea salt and black pepper
1 bunch fresh parsley, finely chopped	

Cook the mushrooms and onions in the butter until they are soft. Pour into a mixing bowl and add the rest of the ingredients for the stuffing. Clean the fish thoroughly and pack in the stuffing, place on a well buttered piece of foil, sprinkle with seasoning and tie up the foil parcel. Bake in a preheated oven at 400°F/200°C/Gas Mark 6 for 30 minutes, and serve on a large platter with lemon and parsley.

Salmon

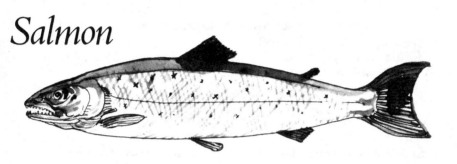

The king of fishes, but sadly at the moment fresh wild salmon is in the decline, which is why when it is in season in the summer months it is expensive. It is in decline because of river pollution (the salmon can only survive in the cleanest of waters) and because of new dams and barriers in rivers which block the salmon's way to their old spawning grounds. There are now salmon farms and farmed salmon are widely available all the year round, they are also much lower in price than the wild salmon. But their flesh tends to be less dense and tightly packed and has a thin layer of fat beneath the skin. The flabbiness is caused by lack of exercise and their flavour leaves a lot to be desired.★ But farmed salmon are good for home smoking, for marinating and eating raw, for barbecuing and for making pâtés, quiches and potted salmon. For such dishes wild salmon would be an extravagance.

Salmon can be bought whole or by weight or in cutlets. A whole salmon is best poached or baked in foil. As most of us do not have vast fish kettles, it is best to bake the fish in foil using plenty of butter and fresh herbs – tarragon and dill are especially good. Bake in a cool oven 300°F/275°C/Gas Mark 2, allowing 12 minutes per pound weight of fish.

Salmon can be a dry fish so if you buy part of one, the tail piece is the moistest. This can be poached in a fish fumet. Bring the fumet to the boil with the fish in it and let it simmer for 5 minutes with the lid on the saucepan. Turn

★It would only be fair to mention that my experience that farmed salmon is inferior to wild is not shared by some of my colleagues. Paul Levy tested pieces of farmed and wild salmon with Prue Leith, and they were in agreement that they found no discernible difference. I can only conclude that they were fortunate in buying salmon from a superior fish farm.

off the heat and let it stay in the fumet for a further 20 minutes. Test that the fish is done with the point of a knife to see whether the flesh comes away from the backbone with ease, if not bring it to the boil for another 2 minutes. The poached fish is traditionally served with hollandaise sauce, new potatoes and either a salad or a garnish of cucumber. Steaks of salmon can also be baked in foil with plenty of butter and herbs. This will ensure that the salmon will never dry out.

Gravlax has become popular in the last few years, it is a side or both sides of marinated salmon and farmed salmon will be excellent with this method. The fishmonger will prepare the salmon for you, for it has to be cleaned, scaled, deboned and bisected lengthways.

Gravlax

1 farmed salmon, prepared as above
4 tablespoons sea salt
2 tablespoons castor sugar
2 tablespoons mixed white and black peppercorns
large bunch dill, chopped
1 glass brandy

Lay one side of the fish, skin side down in a glass dish. Combine all the ingredients except the brandy and rub them into the fish, then pour over the brandy, cover with the other side of the salmon, skin side up. Find a weight to place on top of the fish and refrigerate for three days, turning the fish over every 12 hours and basting with the juices.

Slice the salmon as if it were smoked, scraping off the salt mixture. Traditionally it should be served with a mustard sauce but it seems to me to be perfect without anything.

Because of its cost most of us will buy salmon as cutlets for grilling. Here is another method, where the fish is wrapped in spinach leaves and baked in the oven.

Salmon in Spinach Parcels

4 cutlets of salmon
8 large spinach leaves
bunch of dill
juice from one lemon
butter for greasing the dish
sea salt and freshly ground black pepper

Blanch the spinach leaves and chop the dill finely. Lay each cutlet of salmon on top of a spinach leaf (you may need two, it depends upon the size of the cutlet and the leaf), season well with sea salt and freshly ground black pepper, then cover generously with the chopped dill. Wrap the leaf around the fish so that it is completely covered. Butter an oven dish. Preheat the oven to 400°F/200°C/ Gas Mark 6. Lay the spinach parcels in the oven dish and cover with foil. Place in the oven for 25 minutes.

Can be substituted in:
Roulade de Lotte, page 26
Roast Eels with Apple and Cider, pages 36–7
Filets de Sole Véronique, pages 40–41
Flounder à la Deauvillaise, pages 41–42
Flétan au Poivre, page 48
Roes with Green Peppercorns and Cream, page 50
Dory in Cider and Cream, pages 51–2
Gratin of Scampi and Avocado, page 105
Soufflé, page 123
Creamed Prawns and Rice, page 101
Or cooked as the two recipes for salmon trout, page 82
If plainly cooked, many of the herb butters, mayonnaises and sauces in Chapter IX are suitable.

Salmon Trout

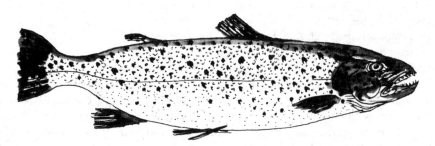

In season between February and August. If fishmongers do not have them, they will generally order them for you. In my opinion these are the best fish of all. Their flavour lies somewhere between wild trout and wild salmon; they are in fact the sea-going version of the wild brown trout. They are roughly 40cm (16 inches) long and any of the trout or salmon recipes are suitable.

I have such regard for this fish that I would only bake it in foil or poach it gently and I think that it is best eaten cold with a sharp fruit sauce as in the recipe below.

Poached Salmon Trout with Redcurrant Sauce

1 salmon trout weighing between
   1.5 and 2kg (3 and 4lbs)

900ml (1½pt) court-bouillon (see
   page 21)

For the sauce

450g (1lb) redcurrants
1 tablespoon castor sugar

pinch of sea salt

Place the cleaned prepared fish into a pan full of the simmering court-bouillon, put a lid on the pan and let it simmer for 5 minutes then turn off the heat and leave for 20 minutes. In the meantime make the sauce. Wash and strip the stalks from the redcurrants and place them in a pan with sugar and salt. Bring to the boil, put the lid on the pan and turn off the heat. Carefully take the fish from its pan, lay it on a platter and peel off the skin. Purée most of the redcurrants through a sieve, return to the pan, give the sauce a stir and pour it around the fish.

Truite-saumonée en Croûte

1 salmon trout weighing between
   1.5 and 2kg (3 and 4lb)
450g (1lb) puff pastry
3 tablespoons finely chopped
   tarragon

sea salt and freshly ground black
   pepper
1 beaten egg
50g (2oz) butter

Leave the head and tail on the fish but carefully skin it. Roll out the pastry to the fish's length so that it will encase it completely. Sprinkle the upper side of the pastry with chopped tarragon and season it. Dice the butter and place half of it on the underside. Lay the fish on the pastry, dot with the remainder of the butter, and carefully fold the pastry over to cover it completely. Use some of the beaten egg to stick the ends together. Use the trimmings to make a design on the top of the fish and paint with the beaten egg. Place carefully on a baking sheet and bake in the preheated oven, at 400°F/200°C/Gas Mark 6, for about 35 minutes or until the pastry is golden brown.

Can be substituted for any of the salmon recipes, pages 79–81. Soufflé, page 123. If plainly cooked, many of the herb butters, mayonnaises and sauces in Chapter IX are suitable.

Trout

It is a sad fact that the wild brown trout hardly ever appears in the shops. The trout that does is the rainbow trout which is farmed. These are widely available and of course in season all the year round.

Their quality depends on the fish farm and the type of feed they have consumed. Some feed has more additives in it than others and the fish grow at a faster rate. Some of these trout can be fatty and tasteless. Their flesh can also be pink, which is not a new species of trout but is entirely due to colouring added to the feed. There is no way of telling whether the farmed trout on the fishmonger's slab is going to be good to eat or not. Only by tasting it can you tell. If it is disappointing tell your fishmonger and try to persuade him not to buy from that fish farm again.

Trout can be grilled, fried, baked in foil or without. The most famous recipe is trout with almonds, a dish I have never seen the point of, as in my view the almonds do not help the fish one bit. In this recipe the cleaned prepared fish is dipped first in milk, then in seasoned flour, then in beaten eggs then rolled in ground almonds, then fried in clarified butter and the trout is served with lemon. But trout can also be smoked, barbecued and eaten raw after marinating for a day. These last methods are all good for the farmed trout, in fact they are rejuvenated by the latter process which works superbly with farmed salmon too and make a marvellous first course. Here is that recipe, and a cooked one from Wales.

Marinated Raw Trout

4 farmed trout, skinned and
   filleted

For the Marinade

juice and zest of 2 oranges	1 tsp. white pepper
juice and zest of 1 lemon	1 tablespoon chopped dill
1 tablespoon sea salt	37.5cl (½ bottle) dry white wine
1 tablespoon castor sugar	

Mix all the marinade ingredients together and pour into a shallow bowl. Slice the fish fillets thinly across in bite-sized slivers. Lay the fish in the marinade. Make sure the fish is covered and leave for 24 hours. Serve with brown bread and butter. Excellent with farmed salmon too.

Welsh Trout

4 trout	8 rashers smoked streaky bacon*
sea salt and black pepper	1 tablespoon juniper berries

Choose a casserole to fit the amount of fish. Season the cleaned prepared fish and wrap each one round with two rashers of bacon. Fit them into the casserole head to tail. Crush the juniper berries and sprinkle them over the top. Put the lid on the casserole and bake in a preheated oven at 350°F/180°C/Gas Mark 4 for 20 minutes.

Can be substituted in:
Filets de Sole Véronique, pages 40–41
Flounder à la Deauvillaise, pages 41–2
Flétan au Poivre, page 48
Roes with Green Peppercorns and Cream, page 50
Dory in Cider and Cream, pages 51–2
Turbot with Crab Sauce, page 66
French method with Whiting, page 68
Also good cold in mixed fish salads.
If plainly cooked, many of the herb butters, mayonnaises and sauces in Chapter IX are suitable.

*See note on dry sow stalls on page 49.

CHAPTER IV

SHELLFISH

'He was a bold man that first eat an oyster.'
Jonathan Swift,
Polite Conversation, dialogue 2.
(1738)

Clams

There are several varieties in the species, but only three varieties are found in British waters. More are found on the French side of the English Channel and the Channel Islands. In these islands you can eat a dish of *fruits de mer* as good as any in the world and there will be several types of clam included. The clams you will find in British waters are the carpet shell, the venus shell and the hard shell which exists in a colony in Southampton Water. The latter is also known as the quahog and is the clam used in Manhattan Clam Chowder.

Clams are for the most part eaten raw like oysters. Choose only undamaged ones and discard any that are open. Put the point of a knife into the hinge at the back of the clam and cut through the muscle, forcing the top shell up. Serve the clam in the bottom shell with lemon juice, pepper and Tabasco. Alternatively, clams may be steamed until they open, then eaten with melted butter. The best clams I have had were in Senegal, when we cut the roots of the trees that hung down in the river, these we piled up in the boat and took back to land, where we made a fire, and laid the roots, encrusted with clams, over the fire. In the damp and the heat they steamed open and as they opened we ate them.

Clams can also be stuffed and then grilled; use any stuffing for baked fish. You can also purchase clam juice in cans which is useful in soups and stews. Clams themselves are also useful, as are cockles and winkles, as an ingredient in soups and stews. They are, however, most famous as the main ingredient in Clam Chowder.

Clam Chowder

3 dozen clams
225g (8oz) salt pork★
3 onions, sliced
450g (1lb) tomatoes
450g (1lb) leeks, cleaned and
  sliced (see page 184)
450g (1lb) potatoes, peeled and
  chopped
2 bay leaves
pinch of nutmeg

½ tsp. sea salt
50g (2oz) butter
50g (2oz) flour
6 water biscuits
2 tablespoons finely chopped
  parsley
1 tablespoon Worcestershire
  sauce
½ tsp. Tabasco
300ml (½pt) single cream

Dice the salt pork and put it in a large saucepan with the sliced onions; cook
them together over a low heat for 10 minutes. In another pan place the cleaned
clams and cover them with water. Bring them to the boil and throw away any
that have not opened. Cut the clams from the shells and chop them up small.
Place these in the pan with the pork and add the peeled and seeded tomatoes,
the leeks and the potatoes, the bay leaves, nutmeg and seasoning. Pour in the
water that the clams have cooked in and simmer for 20 minutes. Take out the
bay leaves.

In a bowl mix the softened butter with the flour (*beurre manié*); crumble
the water biscuits and add them both to the chowder. The *beurre manié* will
have to be added in small pellets, so that the soup slowly absorbs the flour.
Add also the parsley, the Worcestershire sauce and Tabasco. Lastly add the
single cream, stir well and serve piping hot.

★See note on page 49.

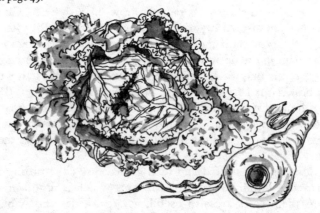

Cockles

Cockles live around our shores buried in the sand around the low tide mark. They have to be washed by immersion in clean water when they will clean themselves of the grains of sand they have accumulated.

Every major seaside resort sells them fresh from stalls where they are eaten raw. They are eaten with a pin, the hard disc at their opening being first pierced and thrown away. Then the cockle is extracted, they are seasoned with pepper and vinegar and eaten with buttered brown bread. They can be cooked too; throw them into a dry pan and put over a flame. When they open they are cooked, and they can then be added to soups and stews.

Crab

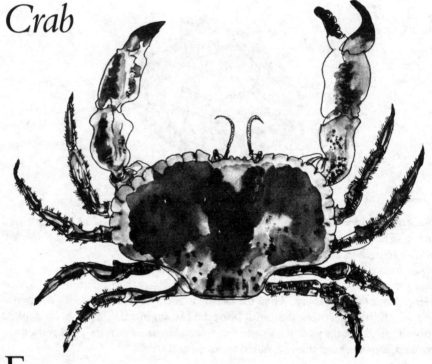

Fresh crab can often be bought from fishing ports, particularly on the east and south-west coast and west Wales. It can also be bought in good fishmongers and large food stores. Its season is from May to October.

Frozen crab and frozen dressed crab is widely available. Freezing does something terrible to the flesh of shellfish, it makes it watery and tasteless. (If there are exceptions to this, I have not come across them nor have any of my friends.) If dressed crab is frozen by your local fishmonger to keep for a few days, little harm is done and there is little difference from the fresh. It is the frozen crab which is stored for some time that appears to be ruined.

Tinned crab is also no good for cooking and it makes a poor substitute for fresh crab in a salad. There are also crab sticks, these are mostly white fish mixed with a little crab and then given crab flavouring.

Fresh crab has been boiled which accounts for its pinkness. Live crab can be occasionally bought, though you have no way of telling how long the crabs have been kept in the tanks. You also have the delicate problem of killing the creature. Plunge the crab in boiling salted water for ten minutes then simmer for another twenty and leave to cool. Alan Davidson gives a humane way of killing crabs by sticking an awl into its brain and nervous centre – two different spots – but I have no intention of holding a struggling crab down while I search for these precise spots. The crab is hardly going to hold the book up for me at the right page.

Extracting the flesh from a crab is a fiddly business, but think how superb the result will be. Fresh crab is absurdly cheap, if it is dressed, you pay double the price, so it is worth getting practice in.

Lay the cooked crab on its back, press down, push forward and then prise up with the thumbs, and the whole body with the legs will come free of the carapace. (Or you can pull the legs off first.) Press on the small mouth part and it will snap away. Discard this with the stomach and the gills (called 'dead men's fingers'). All of the rest of the meat can be eaten. Put the brown meat in one bowl and the white meat in another.

The males have large claws and have more white meat. Crack the claws with a small hammer and the fish will pull out. The small legs can be broken and the flesh extracted with a larding needle or thin skewer.

The most common way of eating crab is to mix it with fresh herbs, a sauce, a little flavouring, or a mayonnaise and enjoy it with a mixed salad. All the flesh can be served packed back into the shell. (Wash the shell thoroughly before using it as a serving plate.) Keep the white and brown meat separate, their flavour is quite different.

You can make croquettes, by adding breadcrumbs and rolling them in egg, flour and a few breadcrumbs.

Crab and sweetcorn soup is one of the great soups of the world (see page 149). Or the flesh can be mixed with a sauce, Mornay, Béchamel or Hollandaise or any variation and served with rice.

Crab mixed with a little sauce in pastry tartlets is excellent.

Crab can be used instead of angler fish for the recipe Roulade de Lotte (page 26). Mix the flesh of a large crab with 150ml (5fl oz) of sour cream and a generous handful of chopped parsley and chives. Spread this on the puff pastry and continue as for that recipe. It is a sumptuous feast.

Dressed Crab

meat from 3 crabs
75g (3oz) cream cheese
sea salt and freshly ground black
    pepper
parsley and lemon for garnish

2 tablespoons each of finely
    chopped chives, parsley and
    basil
zest and juice from 1 lemon

Mix all the brown meat with the rest of the ingredients in a bowl. Pile back into the shells, decorate the top with the white meat and then garnish with the parsley and lemon.

Serve with a green salad.

Note: there are many variations. Use also mayonnaise, horseradish, cream, sour cream, fromage frais or quark, to moisten and bind the crab meat.

Crawfish (or spiny lobster)

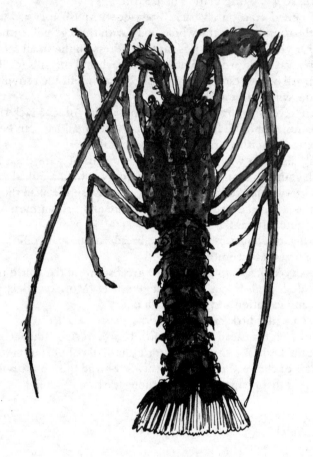

This is the lobster without huge pincer claws. Instead it has two wavy antennae. It is in season from April to September. It is found in south-west England and southern Ireland. The flesh is as good as lobster.

They are deep frozen sometimes within their shells and sold just under the name of lobster. They look like a long red roll. Never buy them, the flesh is tasteless and completely inedible. If you are lucky enough to find a fresh one which has been boiled, prepare and cook the flesh as for lobster. Most of the fresh ones caught here and elsewhere in Europe are flown to Paris. In France these are called *langouste*.

Crayfish

These are small freshwater lobsters about 7.5 to 10cm (3 to 4 inches) long. They are never found in the shops, but an angler may still catch one or two by mistake. They only thrive in clean, well oxygenated water and exist near the banks of streams.★

To cook, boil in court-bouillon for ten minutes, allow to cool, split open (see lobster) take out tiny sac and gut, then fry in butter, or eat the flesh cold with a sauce.

You will find them in France, however, where they are the main part of the famous Nantua sauce. If you see that magic name on the menu, as in *quenelles de brochet Nantua*, choose it, and you will find your pike quenelles sitting in a creamy sauce and garnished with one whole crayfish. The sauce is made from crayfish butter, which is shell and flesh poached and blended into butter with béchamel sauce and cream added.

Crayfish, or *écrevisse*, appear in the fishmarkets in France as well as on the menu. All the recipes for prawns, scampi and lobster are suitable.

★Zoologists have recently become worried because the native British species has had an alien invader from America which has brought a disease with it which affects the British crayfish and they are now on the decline. The American species is also edible.

Lobster

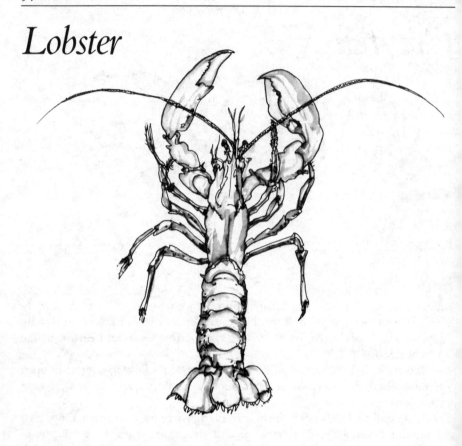

The most loved of the crustacea and one of the great delicacies of the table. Found all around the British coasts, it is in season from April to October.

Buy lobsters freshly boiled, not live from tanks with their claws tied, as they are likely to be in poor condition. Most British lobsters are exported or go straight to restaurants.

Lobsters may seem expensive but it is no more than steak, and it is healthier to eat as it has minimal saturated fat. Buy one weighing between 675 and 900g (1½ and 2lb), as the larger the lobster the less flavour. With a small lobster there is only enough meat for one person.

To prepare a lobster, lay it on its back and insert the point of a strong sharp knife between the body and the tail. Cut down the tail to the end, bisecting it completely. Then cut the body in two in the same way. Take out the thread of dark gut which runs down the tail, and the gristly pouch of grit at the top of the head. The creamy part and the green substance (the liver, tomalley) can be picked out and added to the sauce, also the coral and any liquor from inside the lobster. Alternatively you can mix all this with the sliced parts of the tail. Crack the claws and take out the meat. It is best then to take out all the flesh, prepare it in the way you want and return it to the shell.

The most popular way of eating lobster is to consume it cold with a mayonnaise or a sauce. Take the flesh from the tail, slice it, mix it with a sauce and replace it in the shell. Or the lobster can be served sliced as above with the sauce in a separate bowl.

If you want to eat your lobster hot, after slicing it and preparing it, paint the lobster meat with butter and place under a hot grill for a few minutes. Serve with a hollandaise sauce. Most of the classic dishes with lobster I find inappropriate; tossing the diced flesh in brandy, or laying a creamy sauce over it all is gilding the lily. Lobster is so good that it should be enjoyed in a simple way. I also find mayonnaise and hollandaise too rich for the succulence of the flesh. (But for readers who do not agree with me, there is a list of recipes below which are rich enough to satiate any gourmand.)

Alexandre Dumas in his *Dictionary of Cuisine* cooks live lobsters by plunging them into boiling salted water, which also has butter, parsley, a red pepper, 2 or 3 stalks of leek and a glass of madeira in it. He allows the lobster to cool in this liquid and serves it with the following sauce.

Alexandre Dumas' Sauce for Lobster

1 tablespoon Dijon mustard	2 finely chopped shallots
12 drops of soy sauce	pepper
1 tablespoon each of finely chopped parsley, chives, tarragon and basil	1 glass of anise
	juice of 2 lemons
	150ml (¼pt) olive oil

Mix all the ingredients together thoroughly, then fold the chopped lobster flesh into the dressing.

This is all very well, but personally I like a chunk of lobster that is not soaked in sauce now and again, in fact, I like the choice to be mine, whether to dunk in sauce or not. As I also think all the usual sauces are too rich here is my alternative.

Spencer's Sauce for Lobster

flesh from a ripe avocado	1 tablespoon each of finely chopped tarragon and chives
65ml (2½fl oz) sour cream	
65ml (2½fl oz) yoghurt	½ tsp. sea salt
1 tsp. crushed green peppercorns	juice and zest from one lemon

Take the flesh from the avocado and place in the blender jar. Add all the rest of the ingredients and blend to a thick smooth purée. Taste and check for seasoning, before scooping it out and into a bowl.

Can also be substituted in:
Roulade of Crab, page 91
Filets de Sole Véronique, pages 40–41
Roes with Green Peppercorns and Cream, page 50
Dory in Cider and Cream, pages 51–2
Creamed Prawns and Rice, page 101
Poached Scallops in White Wine, page 103
Gratin of Scampi and Avocado, page 105
Truite-saumonée en Croûte, page 82
Baked Giant Prawns with Garlic, page 134
Swordfish with Croutons, page 139
If plainly boiled or steamed, both Anchovy and Watercress Butters (page 167) are suitable, as are all of the mayonnaises (pages 168–9). Herb (page 171), Tomato (page 171), Caper (page 173) or Green Peppercorn Sauce (page 173) can also be used.

Mussels

These grow in abundance all around our shores. They are in season from September to April. For the most part we avoid molluscs in the summer months because this is their breeding season, but also because in the warm weather toxic micro-organisms can flourish. All molluscs feed by pumping water through their shells and taking out the plankton; if they are feeding in polluted water or near a chemical waste outlet then they will be building up poisons within themselves.

One of the great pleasures of life is to collect mussels at low tide by yourself. All you must remember is to choose a spot where they are abundant and where you know the water is clean. The last time I did this was in a bay in southern Ireland where the mussels were huge and hanging in clusters on the rocks and breakwaters. I filled three buckets and we had a huge cauldron of *moules marinières*.

There are now on sale plastic bags of cleaned mussels; these are fresh and as good as the others, they just save you the chore of cleaning them. But this I have never found an especial chore. Use a knife and not a brush and simply scrape away the barnacles from the shells under a cold running tap. Throw away any cracked mussel, or any that is open, even if merely a crack is showing (or tap the mussel that is just slightly open and if it snaps back shut, the mussel is alive and well and can be eaten). When all the mussels are clean, you boil them in water and use all the mussels that opened. You throw away the ones that are still shut – very few if any at all. But these are the golden rules to remember. Once the mussels are cooked, you can stuff them in their half shells and pop them under a grill, or you can use them in other dishes to add flavour.

Mussels with Herb Butter

allow 10–12 mussels per person
225g (8oz) softened butter
2 shallots, finely chopped
3 cloves of garlic, crushed
3 tablespoons dry white wine

3 tablespoons chopped parsley
sea salt and freshly ground black
  pepper
50g (2oz) gruyère

Scrape the shells of the mussels under running water and throw away any open or damaged ones. With a knife prize open each shell near the hinge, cutting the muscles which hold the shell shut. Throw away one side of the shell, leaving the mussel in the other. Place the softened butter in a bowl and mix in the shallots and garlic. Whisk in the white wine, parsley, seasoning and grated gruyère.

Spoon the herb butter over each mussel in its shell and place the shells on a baking tray. Preheat the oven to 400°F/200°C/Gas Mark 6 and cook the mussels for 5 minutes or until the butter begins to bubble.

See soups and stews (Chapter VII) and salads (page 105) for uses for mussels. Can be substituted for prawns in avocados (see page 82), or egg and breadcrumbed as for scallops (see page 102), or mixed with other fish in tartlets and pies. All the herb butters in Chapter IX are suitable as stuffing for grilled mussels.

Oysters

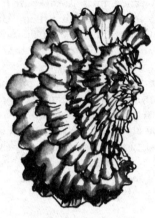

European Oyster

Pacific Oyster

These live in shallow coastal waters and have been eaten since the earliest days of man, as we know from their shells found in ancient settlements. The Romans first cultivated them and started oyster farms in British coastal waters which still exist. The most famous is the Colchester Oyster, but others are from Whitstable, Helford in Cornwall and the Blackwater estuary in Essex.

Oysters are unique in that throughout their life they change sex according to their feeding conditions and the temperature of the water. They can live for 20 to 30 years but they are eaten in their third or fourth year. They are males in the colder waters and become females in the summer when they give birth. It is for this reason that oysters are not caught in the summer months.

In Autumn 1983, the native British oyster beds were struck by a disease called bonamia (which does not affect humans) which has already infected the European oyster beds. But even before this had occurred, the Pacific oyster had been introduced. The Pacific oyster is larger and can be eaten throughout the year for they breed very well in commercial hatcheries as opposed to the beds in river estuaries. These oysters are excellent for cooking because their flavour becomes more pronounced when cooked. You find now many Chinese restaurants that have deep fried oysters on the menu. These are the Pacific ones, succulent and delicious; they will soon be on the supermarket shelves as a regular feature.

The native oyster will have recovered from bonamia in two to three years time. The best cure has always been to let the oyster beds become fallow for five years.

Oysters are nearly always eaten raw with lemon juice, cayenne pepper or

Tabasco. After eating the oysters the liquor in the shell is sipped. Cultivated oysters tend to be expensive and therefore are rarely cooked. But if wild oysters are caught in any numbers, they can be steamed open like mussels and made into a soup. This is a rare treat for they are amazingly good (follow recipe for *moules marinières*, page 150–51). Oysters can also be plainly grilled with the addition of a little herb butter, but they must be hardly cooked at all, merely allow the edges to curl up a little. Tins of smoked oysters can be purchased in most delicatessens. Though good there is little difference in flavour to smoked mussels so it is not worth paying the extra price for the oyster.

Angels on Horseback

8 oysters
8 rashers of smoked back bacon★
4 slices of wholemeal toast

butter for spreading
sea salt and freshly ground black
  pepper

Open the oysters by sticking a strong knife into the back of the oyster near where the muscle holds the shells together. Slice the muscle and prise the shell open. Save the liquor but take each oyster out and roll it in the bacon. Butter the toast and keep warm while you pop the oysters beneath the grill. Cook just so that the bacon is done, turning them over, then add the liquor to the bacon fat and let that sizzle a little beneath the grill, while you arrange two oysters on each piece of toast, then pour the liquor in the grillpan over each Angel on Horseback. Serve at once.

See mussels for alternative ways of cooking.

★See note on page 49.

Prawns

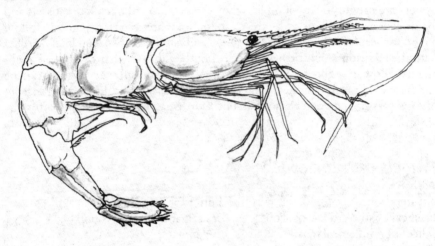

These are widely available and in season all the year round. They are on sale already boiled and can be bought by the pint.

Most of the prawns on sale come from deep waters off Norway, *Pandalus Borealis*; some are prawns from British inshore waters, *Palaemon serratus*. In France these are called *crevette nordique* and *crevette rose*, but they refer to both as *crevettes* as we call ours just prawns, for there is little difference in the look or the flavour. The northern prawn tends to be rather larger and they are red in life as well as after they are boiled, which happens on the fishing fleet at sea. Our common prawn, when it is alive, is quite colourless, reflecting the sand or rocks around it. Only when it is boiled does it turn a bright orangy red. Both prawns are delicious to eat.

You can also buy prawns already peeled, or frozen and peeled. I would avoid both. The frozen peeled prawns taste a bit doughy and the sea seems an infinity away. The freshly peeled prawns taste much better and are worthy of a good brown bread sandwich, but you miss all the goodness and the liquor that one gets from the head and shells.

Both prawns and shrimps are highly nutritious. They are the scavengers of the sea and act in a large group like the ants on land, to reduce any dead object to a few bones in a very short time.

Prawns are generally eaten cold as a salad, or used to stuff avocados. But there are many more exciting things to do with them and certainly if you use the shells, it is best to eat your prawns hot. Even if they are used as a salad, the prawn liquor from the shells and from the heads can be mixed into a dressing and the flavour will be that much more intensified.

Globe Artichokes stuffed with Prawns

4 large globe artichokes
1.75l (3pts) prawns
juice and zest from 1 lemon
2 egg yolks

225ml (7fl oz) olive oil
sea salt and freshly ground black
   pepper

Peel the prawns, and place the shells into a saucepan, squeeze the juice from the heads over the prawns and put the heads into the pan as well. Cover with water, the zest and lemon juice and simmer for 15 minutes. Leave to cool.

Meanwhile, snip the top of the leaves from the artichokes and boil them in salted water for 40 minutes, or until they are tender. Take from the water and leave to drain. When they are cool, pluck out the central leaves, and dig out the choke, exposing the bottom beneath. Throw the central leaves and choke away.

Blend the prawn shell and water and pour through a sieve. Boil the water and reduce to two tablespoons. Let it cool. Mix the two egg yolks together and start adding the oil drop by drop to make mayonnaise, beating all the time. Continue until the oil is used up. The mayonnaise should be very thick. Season it and beat into it the prawn liquor. Now add all the prawns and their juices to the mayonnaise, mix well and pile into the artichoke shells.

Creamed Prawns and Rice

1.75l (3pts) prawns
juice and zest from 1 lemon
100g (4oz) Patna rice
40g (1½oz) unsalted butter

handful of finely chopped parsley
65g (2½oz) thick cream
sea salt and freshly ground black
   pepper

Peel the prawns and boil the shells as for above, using the lemon. Blend the shells and sieve them. Reduce the liquor to 150ml (5fl oz) and season it, then add the chopped parsley.

Meanwhile cook the rice and dry it out in a very low oven for 5 minutes. Cook the prawns for a moment in the butter in a frying pan, then pour over the liquor and parsley, let this bubble away for a minute or two, then stir in the cream, season and bring it back to the heat.

Turn out the rice onto a platter and fashion it into a ring, pour the prawns in their sauce into the centre and serve.

Can be substituted in the scallop and scampi recipes (pages 103 and 105)
Also in Soufflé, page 123
Baked Giant Prawns with Garlic, page 134
See the recipes for soups, stews and fish pies in Chapter VII for other uses.
Prawns are also used in terrines and mousses as well as for garnishing.

Scallops

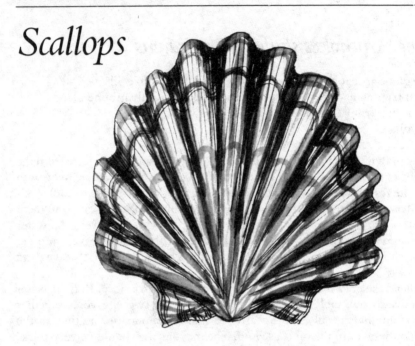

These live around our coasts and are fished by dredging off the seabed. Most are exported. In season from September to April. They are easily recognized because the scallop shell has been used in decoration since ancient times. The most famous representation being Botticelli's *Birth of Venus*, where the golden girl is about to step ashore from a scallop shell that is obviously not quite big enough to contain her.

The shells used to be very common with the scallop lying upon its bed on the fishmonger's marble slab. But now fresh scallops are sold without their shells. This is because scallops are sold by weight and the weight of the shell is as much or more than its contents. Sadly, the shells are thrown back into the sea.

Frozen scallops are widely available too, but they are a waste of money, freezing, as with all shellfish, takes all the flavour out of them. Much better to buy a fresh sprat.

Scallops need very little cooking. There are countless classic recipes. Allow 3 or 4 scallops to each person. But the one the British always adore is to flour, egg and breadcrumb the scallops and to place them in a pan where several rashers of smoked bacon have been cooking. The scallops then fry in the bacon fat for a few minutes, just until they are crisp and light golden brown on the outside.

Some people like to fry the whole scallop with the coral, others will cook the coral separately. As the coral often comes easily away, it is best to cook it gently on its own.

Scallops *en brochette* is another popular way of cooking them. They will barbecue beautifully. Take a large skewer and alternate a piece of scallop with bacon, green pepper, tomato or mushroom. Brush the skewers with olive oil which has salt, pepper and crushed garlic in it. Barbecue over fennel twigs. Or they can be simply grilled.

Another way of grilling them is to slice the white part down the centre, so that you have two discs, then butter a grill pan and lay the scallops with the coral in the pan with several chopped cloves of garlic on top. Cover with more pats of butter and plenty of seasoning. Grill for about five minutes. There is no need to turn them. Yet scallops and dry white wine, especially Muscadet, go so well together that it is difficult not to cook them in any other way.

Poached Scallops in White Wine

12 scallops
37.5cl (½ bottle) Muscadet
40g (1½oz) unsalted butter
25g (1oz) plain flour
½ tsp. lemon juice

sea salt and freshly ground black
  pepper
1 tablespoon chopped tarragon
150ml (5fl oz) thick cream

Divide the coral from the white meat. Pour the wine into a saucepan, add the white meat and simmer for 5 minutes, then add the coral and simmer for another 5 minutes.

Make a roux with the butter and the flour, pour in the liquor the scallops have cooked in and make a smooth sauce. Add the lemon juice and seasoning and then the tarragon. Beat in the cream. When the sauce is smooth and thick, place the scallops onto a dish and pour the sauce over them.

Can be substituted (remembering that they only need brief cooking) in:
Lotte Provençale, page 26
Filets de Sole Véronique, pages 40–41
Flétan au Poivre, page 48
Roes with Green Peppercorns and Cream, page 50
Plaice with Coriander Butter, page 56
Skate with Capers, page 62
Clam Chowder, page 88
Creamed Prawns and Rice, page 101
Gratin of Scampi and Avocado, page 105
Soufflé, page 123
If plainly poached, any of the herb butters may be used, and these sauces: Mornay (page 170), Cream (page 170), Anchovy (page 170), Herb (page 171), Fennel (page 171), Tomato (page 171), Caper (page 173), Walnut (page 174), and Tarragon (page 174).

Scampi

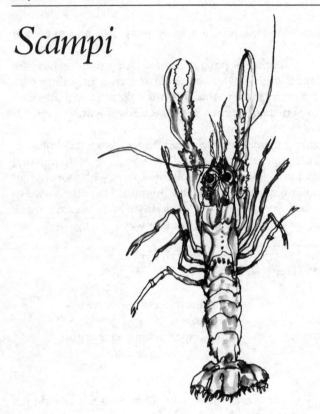

This used to be called Dublin Bay Prawn and its correct name is Norway Lobster. The French call it *langoustine*. Scampi is the Italian plural of their name (*scampo*).

Scampi are found in south-west Ireland and the Scottish coast. They are also found in seas as far away as Iceland and the Adriatic, where they are particular favourites of the Venetians.

The name Dublin Bay Prawn comes from the fact that the Irish fishing boats would reach Dublin Bay with their fish and the prawns were given to the fishermen as being worthless, they in turn gave them to the Dublin street vendors.

These prawns are now a highly prized catch and there is a scampi industry off the coast of Scotland.

On the Continent you can buy scampi alive or cooked but always whole; they value the heads and shells in their cooking. In Britain you almost never see them on sale whole or uncooked. They are separated from the head and claws, and the tails are frozen. At this stage they are worth cooking. But generally there is a further stage, when the tails are thawed, shelled and refrozen. These are how you will find them in the supermarkets. I don't think these are worth doing anything with.

Of course, the next stage in food manufacture is when these tasteless lumps are covered in breadcrumbs and are refrozen again. Sometimes they are plunged in a heavy batter and marketed. This is anathema to a good palate.

In France, all along the Atlantic coast, you will get scampi as part of the *fruits de mer*. A huge round platter filled with oysters, mussels, clams, cockles, whelks, warty venus, crabs, *crevettes* and the scampi, 12 to 15cm (5 to 6 inches) long, crouched upon the seaweed garnish, ready to be shelled and dipped into the lemon mayonnaise. This is how scampi should be eaten. Freshly boiled and shelled by yourselves and dipped into a sauce. But what chance have we when the food manufacturers dictate to us what is good and what we are supposed to think is the most delicious food through the insidious vulgarity of television advertising.

The simplest method of cooking the shelled tails is to toss them in butter and garlic over a medium flame letting them just get crisp, and eat them with rice.

Or use a Venetian method and fry the scampi in olive oil with garlic and then add a few capers, chopped parsley and some lemon juice. Serve the scampi in this sauce.

All the classic methods of cooking lobster can also be used for scampi. But here is a recipe of mine, which is rich but simple. Mediterranean prawns would do instead of the scampi.

Gratin of Scampi and Avocado

675g (1½lb) shelled scampi tails	sea salt and freshly ground black
50g (2oz) butter	pepper
Flesh from 1 ripe avocado	150ml (5fl oz) single cream
pinch of nutmeg	75g (3oz) grated gruyère

Melt the butter in a gratin dish and sauté the scampi in it for 4 to 5 minutes. Dice the flesh from the avocado and stir it into the dish. Add the nutmeg and seasoning, then pour in the cream, stir again and bring it to simmering point. Sprinkle the top with the grated gruyère and pop under a hot grill to brown slightly.

Serve with plain boiled rice.

See alternative recipes to scallops (page 103), Soufflé (page 123).

Shrimp

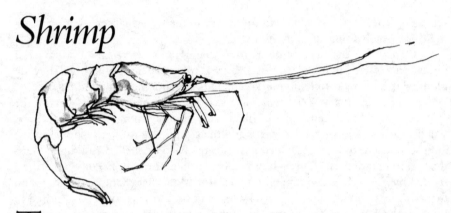

The common brown shrimp is only about 3 to 4cm (1½ inches) long and lives in British inshore waters. It is available all the year round. When you see them in the fishmongers buy a pint or two. They are delicious. Simply snap the head off and eat the rest of the tail, shell and all. If the shells worry you, then take those off, but it is a fiddly process. Nevertheless an excellent sauce can be made from the shells, by just simmering, blending and sieving the liquor.

These shrimps can be potted, by shelling them and cooking them in butter. You can add to the butter and shrimps, when they are cooking, a little nutmeg and cayenne, but do make sure to add plenty of freshly ground black pepper and a pinch of sea salt. You then blend everything together and pour into small pots sealed with clarified butter. They will keep in the refrigerator for ages – months anyway. Mine are never there long enough as they get eaten by passing troops of children. This paste can be spread on toast for breakfast, or be the main part of a sandwich. It is also very useful as an accompaniment for other fish. A pat of homemade shrimp butter on trout or cod makes a lot of difference.

Morecombe Bay has been famous for its shrimps. But the east coast towns of Lowestoft and Felixstowe do not lag far behind. Shrimps can make one of the simplest and the best lunches in the world.

In fishmongers you will also discover pink shrimps, which every fishmonger will stoutly claim are real shrimps. They are in fact prawns, the Baltic prawn which is as small as the brown shrimp. They are just as delicious and can be treated in exactly the same way as the shrimp. Fishmongers often give misnomers to their products and thus help to mystify the public (see monkfish and dogfish).

Can be substituted in the two prawn recipes on page 101, and used in many of the soups, stews and fish pies in Chapter VII. Used as an ingredient in terrines and mousses (pages 162–4) as well as a garnish.
Can be used for stuffing avocadoes and in salads.

Whelks

These are found all around Britain and are sold from stalls with cockles and winkles at most seaside resorts. They are cleaned and boiled and, unless eaten fresh, will be tough. Even when fresh they can be a strenuous chew but their flavour is strong and they are high in protein. They are usually eaten with black pepper and vinegar. In the past they were much used in fish cooking, and sliced they could still be used to flavour soups.

Winkles

The smallest shellfish, sold on stalls along with the cockles and whelks; they are sold ready cooked, in their shells, by the pint. They are not much used in cooking though some adventurous people have added them at the last minute to soups. In Ireland they fry them in bacon fat and then crack two eggs over them. They are best eaten as part of a large *fruits de mer* platter, when they can be extracted with a pin after first dismissing the tiny mica plate, or as a leisurely snack seated on the beach in the sun. Real ale is by far the best drink to have with them.

CHAPTER V

SMOKED AND SALT FISH

'Lord! Let me catch a fish
So large that even I,
In telling of it afterwards,
Shall have no need to lie.'
                                Anon.

Arbroath Smokie

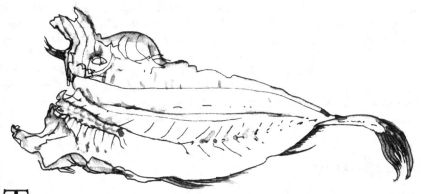

These are small haddock which are smoked in the area of Arbroath in Scotland. They are more widely available in Scotland than in England, but specialist fishmongers always stock them. They are one of the most delicious of all smoked fish and the traditional way of cooking them is to smear them with butter and lightly grill them. They have been hot smoked, so can be eaten cold if you wish.

A word of warning. They will not keep as long as Finnan haddock because they have not been smoked through the depth of the entire fish; if you peel the skin away at the back the flesh will be white and moist. They have no added preservatives and no chemical dyes in them. As a pâté they make an excellent start to a meal with the minimum amount of trouble.

Arbroath Smokie Paté

a pair of Arbroath smokies
75g (3oz) butter, melted
dash Tabasco

pinch sea salt
generous grind of black pepper
1 tablespoon lemon juice

Skin the two fish and bone them; the flesh will flake naturally. Put all of the fish into a blender and add the rest of the ingredients. Blend until you have a thick, smooth purée. Pour into a pot and refrigerate for an hour or more.

They can be used as an ingredient in smoked layered terrines (pages 162–4) and as part of a salad and substituted for Finnan haddock in kedgeree (page 118) and poached with an egg.

Baltic Herring

As its name implies, this way of curing fresh herring comes from Sweden where there are numerous recipes for treating the raw fish. They are exceptionally good and can be purchased in jars, tins and sealed trays. The fish is filleted, salted and placed in a sweet marinade which is flavoured with herbs and spices. They make an excellent first course eaten with salad and brown bread and butter. The marinade can be drained off and mixed with a couple of tablespoons of sour cream and then poured back over the herring fillets. Or you could make your own from fresh herrings as in the recipe below.

Baltic Herring

4 herrings, cleaned, boned,
    skinned and filleted
300ml (½pt) cider vinegar
2 tablespoons sea salt

2 tablespoons muscovado sugar
1 tablespoon pickling spices
2 onions, sliced
1 teaspoon black peppercorns

Lay the herrings in a shallow dish, pour the vinegar into a pan and add all the rest of the ingredients. Bring to the boil and pour over the herrings. Leave for 24 hours. They will keep happily in the refrigerator for a few days. Or if bottled and sealed will keep for months.

Can also be used in mixed fish salads, as garnish and substituted for prawns in avocados and globe artichokes.

Bloater

These are herrings which are not gutted or split but which are immersed in brine for twelve hours and then gently smoked for another twelve hours. They are widely available from any fish shop which specializes in smoked fish. The best bloaters come from Yarmouth and the east coast. Bloaters will also only keep for a few days, as they have been mildly cured. They can be split down the middle, opened out and grilled which is the traditional way of eating them.

They can also be filleted and boned and placed in a marinade and eaten raw. You can also make a bloater paste with the flesh which is excellent on hot brown toast. They can also be boned and skinned and added raw to a potato and onion salad. Any of these last recipes tend at the onset to be fiddly because of the quantity of bones, but once the fish has been split the backbone can be eased up and that will bring most of the smaller bones with it.

Bloater in Mustard Sauce

4 bloaters, skinned, boned and
    filleted
2 tablespoons wholegrain Dijon
    mustard
1 tsp. mustard powder

2 tsp. mixed black and white
    peppercorns
1 tsp. sea salt
2 tsp. brown sugar
300ml (½pt) dry cider

Place the filleted fish in a shallow dish. Mix the rest of the ingredients together, adding the cider last. Pour over the fish and refrigerate for 12 hours. Serve with brown bread and butter.

Can be used in mixed fish salads and substituted for other fish in the marinade recipes. Other suitable sauces are Anchovy (page 170), Curry (page 171), Green Peppercorn (page 173), Horseradish (page 174) and Hot Pepper (page 174).

Buckling

These are unsplit herrings, lightly hot smoked. Therefore they are cooked and like the bloater will not keep for long, even in the refrigerator. They can be grilled and eaten with a herb butter or they can be warmed through in the oven. They can also be eaten cold, like smoked trout, with lemon juice and horseradish sauce. The Danes make a highly delicious pâté out of them that is sold in most delicatessens and specialist fish stores.

See alternative methods for bloater (pages 112–13).

Salt Cod

Available all the year in large specialist food stores and in small ethnic shops, Spanish, Italian, Jewish and Indian.

Spanish and Portugese cuisines have, it is said, over a hundred different recipes for salt cod. The French and Italian cuisines have a number as well with the French *brandade*, for my taste, heading the list. We, of course, have none so must borrow from other countries.

Salt cod can be one of the most delicious experiences in the world and it can also be one of the greatest disappointments. Salt cod looks as if it has been around for years and often it can also look as if it's been used for skate boards.* Don't allow this to put you off trying it. Always buy from a shop which sells its stock steadily and frequently. Buy the fattest pieces and soak for 24 hours, changing the water a couple of times. Then place the cod in cold water, bring to the boil and simmer for 10–15 minutes. Taste the water and if it is too salty throw it away. If not keep for stock or a sauce. As salt cod is highly gelatinous the fish and the liquor it is cooked in will jelly slightly. Let the cod cool a little then bone and skin it. Use the flesh, which should flake easily, for any recipe; the most famous Provençal one is *ailloli garni*, where the cod is served cold with a wide selection of crudités and a huge bowl of garlic mayonnaise. Salt cod goes splendidly with potatoes. One of the best recipes I've made came from Normandy which was with salt cod cheeks, new potatoes and *crème fraîche*, baked in the oven. Salt cod also goes well in various tomato stews, the Spanish love this combination. But it will go splendidly with any form of vegetable stew or baked *en croûte* with herbs and butter in puff pastry.

Brandade

900g (2lb) piece of salt cod	pinch nutmeg
3 cloves garlic, crushed	300ml (½pt) single cream
juice and zest of 1 lemon	450ml (¾pt) olive oil
black pepper	bunch of parsley, finely chopped

Soak the cod for 24 hours then simmer it for 15 minutes. Drain the cod and bone it, but keep the skin which helps the flavour and texture of the *brandade*.

---

*In fourteenth century Paris a fishmonger recommended this treatment for ten-year-old salt cod. 'Beat it with a wooden hammer for a full hour and then set it to soak in warm water for a full two hours or more, then cook it and scour it very well . . . then eat it with mustard or soaked in butter.'

Place the cod in a double saucepan and add the garlic, lemon juice, pepper and nutmeg. With a wooden spoon mix thoroughly and crush the fish and skin together. Gently, in a saucepan, bring the cream to blood heat. In another saucepan do the same with the olive oil. Pour a little oil into the fish, stirring with the wooden spoon so that the fish soaks up the oil, do the same with the cream, go on alternately adding each until oil and cream are finished. You should have something that looks like a soufflé flecked with the black skin. Stir in the chopped parsley. If the *brandade* separates you can pour the whole lot into the electric blender and it should recombine. This is the most heavenly fish purée of them all, excellent with brown toast as a start to a meal. It is also superb in tiny pastry cases as an appetizer.

After the cod has been soaked, poached, skinned and boned, it can be substituted in other recipes as follows:
Lotte Provençal, page 26
Roulade de Lotte, page 26
Marmite, page 31
Fish Croquettes, page 34
Fish Cakes, page 57
Fish Simmered in Ginger and Soy Sauce, page 39
Poached Haddock with Mustard Sauce, pages 45–6
Roes with Green Peppercorns and Cream, page 50
Dory in Cider and Cream, pages 51–2
Turbot with Crab Sauce, page 66
Clam Chowder, page 88
Creamed Prawns and Rice, page 101
Soufflè, page 123
If poached simply, use any of the herb butters or mayonnaises in Chapter IX, also Sauce Bèchamel (page 170), Mornay (page 170), Cream (page 170), Tomato (page 171), Walnut (page 174) and Hot Tomato (page 174).

Smoked Cod

There are in the shops a great deal of yellowish orange fillets of cod which are referred to as smoked. They have been briefly soaked in brine with *tartrazine*, the yellow dye, to give this unappealing and gaudy colour. The fish is then dipped into another solution which gives it a slight smoky flavour. You can sometimes get real smoked cod but it is a fish which smoking does not improve. Even home smoked cod is no great shakes. The only time I would treasure the quality it has is in a mixed fish pie, see Chapter VII.

Smoked Ling

Fillets of ling are also smoked and sold in the fishmongers as smoked cod. There is little difference in the flavour or the quality. And as ling is part of the family of cod the misnomer is hardly serious.

You can now purchase both smoked cod and smoked ling properly smoked, that is without the dyes and additives. The fishmonger that stocks this is naturally proud and so the fish will be clearly marked for what it is. If not, refuse to buy and complain to your fishmonger until he begins to stock properly smoked fish.

Smoked Cod's Roe

Widely available in shops all the year round, this has been growing in popularity in the last few decades. The roes are first salted and then smoked. They can then be eaten, thinly sliced, with lemon juice and wholemeal bread. These slices can also be used in combination with a mixture of smoked and salted fish as a first course.

But it is most renowned in taramasalata, where the roe is skinned and pounded with garlic, lemon juice and olive oil. This is not to be confused with botargo, the salted roes of grey mullet. The taramasalata you buy, made up in delicatessens, or in restaurants, is mixed with white breadcrumbs (or sometimes mashed potato) and artificially coloured flamingo pink. This is an inferior version of the one you can make at home.

Taramasalata

225g (8oz) smoked cod roes
juice and zest of 1 lemon
3 crushed cloves garlic

150ml (¼pt) olive oil
100g (4oz) cream cheese
freshly ground black pepper

Pour boiling water onto the roe and leave for a few seconds. The skin should then peel off easily. Sometimes, it doesn't and you have to scrape the roe off the skin. Put all of the roe into a blender jar and add the juice and zest of the lemon and the garlic. Pour in the oil slowly, as if you were making mayonnaise, so that the roe can absorb it. Then lastly add the cream cheese and the pepper, taste and check for seasoning. Serve with toast or pitta bread.

See Smoked Fish Salad (pages 121–2) for alternative use. When made into a purée like the taramasalata above, it can be used in pastry tartlets, for stuffing avocados instead of prawns, for stuffing globe artichokes.

Smoked Eel

Available in all smoked fish shops and some fishmongers. Buy a portion of the whole eel and skin and fillet it at home. If you buy the fillets already prepared they may have dried out and become tasteless and chewy. The black skin will be as hard as leather but will come away like a glove if you use a pair of pliers. The flesh inside should be moist and firm, not mushy. The centre bone can easily be extracted. Fresh eel will hot smoke at home superbly.

Eat the fillets as a first course with horseradish or mustard sauce or with scrambled eggs. Lightly grill the fillets and eat them as a savoury on toast. Marinate them for a day, but use a light marinade or else it will swamp the delicate flavour.

Marinated Smoked Eel

450g (1lb) smoked eel fillets
2 tsp. sugar
2 tsp. salt
1 tsp. white pepper

juice and zest from 1 lemon
juice and zest from 2 oranges
37.5cl (½ bottle) dry white wine
or dry cider

In a shallow glass dish mix all the ingredients for the marinade together. Lay the fillets in the marinade ensuring that they are all covered. Leave in the refrigerator for a day. The sauce cuts across the fattiness of the eel beautifully. Serve with brown bread and butter.

Use as an ingredient in fish salads, soufflé (page 123), puréed in smoked fish terrines (pages 162–4). Other suitable sauces are Anchovy (page 170), Curry (page 171), Hot Tomato (page 174), Hot Pepper (page 174) and Green Peppercorn (page 173).

Finnan Haddock

With kipper, the most famous of all the smoked fish. They got their name from Findon, a village in Aberdeenshire, which started to salt and smoke haddock in the 1820s. They are a pale golden colour and keep well in a refrigerator for up to a week.

They are generally poached in milk, but I prefer to put them in a saucepan with butter over a very small flame and let them cook in their own steam. There seems no point in putting a delicate smoked flavour into the fish and then cooking it by a process which leaches the flavour out.

Finnan haddocks are easily distinguished as they are split down the middle and still keep their tails. There are other golden haddock fillets which have been dyed.

Another traditional way of eating poached haddock is to top the fish with a poached egg. They are superb as one of the fish in a fish pie, and are the main ingredient in kedgeree, of which I give a simple recipe below.

Kedgeree

900g (2lb) Finnan haddock
100g (4oz) butter
3 hard-boiled eggs
175g (6oz) Patna rice

generous handful chopped
 parsley
sea salt and black pepper
2 beaten eggs

Place 25g (1oz) of the butter into a pan and fish with it, put the lid on the saucepan and place over a low heat for 15 minutes. Leave to cool then bone and skin the fish. Peel and chop the three eggs finely, add these to the fish. Pour some boiling water into a pan and cook the rice, add a little salt and let it simmer until it is just done. Place the rice in a colander and let it dry out in a low oven for 5 minutes. Melt the remaining butter and pour in the fish and egg, add the rice, give everything a good stir over a low heat. Add the parsley and a lot of freshly ground black pepper. When the dish is hot pour in the 2 beaten eggs and stir until they are cooked. Serve at once.

Note: this simple kedgeree is cooked without Indian spices which are required in the original dish.

Can be substituted in the following recipes:
Roulade de Lotte, page 26
Roast Eel with Apples and Cider, pages 36–7
Flounder à la Deauvillaise, pages 41–2

Kipper

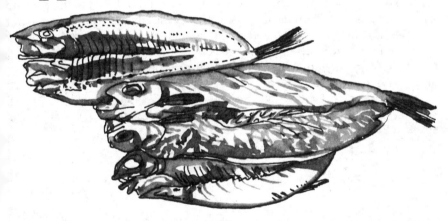

Specialist fishmongers still stock the oak smoked kipper, a fact of life for which I am profoundly grateful. These are available all the year round. What is available in every fishmonger and supermarket in Britain are the kippers which are artificially dyed with Brown FK, a dye which is banned in the rest of the Common Market. The manufacturers claim that the housewife wants her kipper to be a dark mahogany brown. If you have never tasted a naturally smoked kipper buy one and see the difference.

Everyone has their favourite way of preparing kippers; they can be plainly grilled or, as rumour has it, the method the Queen Mother prefers, grilled with a little water in the pan beneath so that the kippers are partially steamed as well. The most elitist way of preparing your kippers is to put them into a large jug, tail down and pour boiling water into the jug, then to leave the jug for five minutes before taking the kippers out and draining them. Kippers can be baked in foil in the oven, they will be done in 10 minutes in a hot oven, or poached in an open pan. They can also be eaten raw with lemon juice and a lot of black pepper. But the dyed ones would taste foul. An excellent pâté can also be made out of the raw flesh or they can be marinated like the bloater. They are also a perfect foil to scrambled egg, which makes one of the best dishes for brunch.

Kipper Fillets with Scrambled Eggs

4 oak smoked kippers
50g (2oz) butter
5 beaten eggs

handful finely chopped parsley
sea salt and black pepper

Poach the 4 kippers in pairs, both together in the pan. Bring a little water to the boil and let them simmer for 2 minutes, then put a lid over the pan and leave for 5 minutes. Drain the kippers well and carefully bone and skin them.

Meanwhile, use half the butter and scramble the eggs, adding the parsley and seasoning. Place the scrambled eggs on a platter while they are still runny. Put the rest of the butter into the pan and turn the kipper fillets in it. Pour them, with their juices, over the eggs.

See alternative methods for Bloater (page 113), Buckling (page 113) and Smoked Eel (page 117).

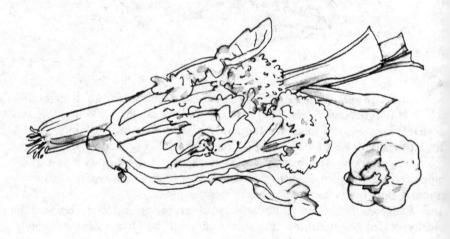

Smoked Mackerel

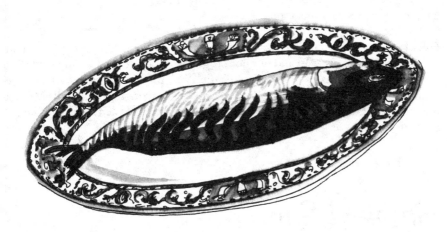

Widely available in most fish shops. The smoked mackerel is a tremendously oily fish so it is very filling and highly nutritious. The large mackerel tend to have flesh which is rather mushy in texture, but these are excellent for making pâtés. If you wish to eat mackerel, either hot or cold, choose the smaller fish which are slightly less fatty. If you have large appetites, allow one fish to each person; they are eaten with horseradish and mustard sauce and brown bread and butter.

These fish can also be filleted and used with a combination of other salted and smoked fish. The whole smoked fish can also be grilled or wrapped in foil and baked. You can now also buy filleted smoked mackerel which saves you the trouble of boning your fish; eat these with plenty of lemon juice. Also on sale are peppered mackerel fillets which seems to be more of a gimmick, than a help to the flavour of the fish, and at 20 pence more per pound cannot be worth it. One of the best dishes is a cold mixed fish salad in pepper sauce using raw and smoked fish. Here the smoked mackerel fillets come into their own. You will occasionally find on sale cold smoked mackerel. These are excellent in any of the marinades and then eaten raw. But thcy can also be grilled.

Smoked Fish Salad

2 fillets smoked mackerel
2 smoked trout
100g (4oz) smoked cod's roe

100g (4oz) raw Scotch wild
   salmon
100g (4oz) prawns

For the sauce

juice and zest of 3 limes
2 tablespoons black peppercorns
2 tablespoons green peppercorns

2 tablespoons walnut oil
½ tsp. Tabasco

Fillet the smoked trout and cut it into 2.5cm (1 inch) pieces. Cut the smoked mackerel in the same way and put both together on a platter, add tiny slivers of the cod's roe and, carefully cutting all the skin, fat and bone away from the salmon, slice the flesh into thin slivers. Add the prawns and mix well. Mix all the ingredients for the sauce together and pour over the salad. Add more lime or lemon wedges as garnish and serve very cold.

Smoked Salmon

Widely available and ranging in quality from the very best with Scottish salmon to Danish tinned smoked salmon. The best salmon is, of course, highly expensive and even that is graded in quality and price. There are now many names in the salmon smoking business and you can also buy imported Canadian smoked salmon. Farmed salmon are also smoked and it is a matter of trying various types until you discover a smoking house whose product you consider the best at a price you can afford. Do not buy salmon already sliced and packaged. Insist on your salmon being sliced for you at the counter, and eat it with lemon, lots of freshly ground black pepper and thin slices of wholemeal bread and butter. The salmon scraps can be used for all manner of dishes. These sell for at least half the price and are useful to make smoked salmon soufflés (see below), quiches and tarts. You can also make good potted salmon from them by placing them in the blender jar with butter and pepper (see page 159). This will keep in the refrigerator for a few months and is a useful standby to have to spread on toast or as a first course instead of pâté. One of the best smoked salmon appetizers is the one below. This does not require the best smoked salmon.

225g (½lb) smoked salmon
1 small brown loaf
butter

75g (3oz) cream cheese
freshly ground black pepper

Carefully slice the crusts from all sides of the loaf then cut long thin slices of bread from the bottom of the loaf, butter them, place smoked salmon over them and be generous with the pepper mill. Now spread a layer of cream cheese over the salmon and carefully roll the bread up from one end. When the roll is tight and neat place in the refrigerator for 30 minutes. Cut the rolls across into 5mm (¼ inch) thicknesses so that they are spirals. These look as good as they taste.

Smoked Salmon Soufflé

225g (8oz) smoked salmon scraps
300ml (½pt) single cream
6 eggs, separated

pinch of cayenne pepper
butter
50g (2oz) gruyère cheese

Reduce the salmon pieces to a rough purée in the blender. Add the single cream and the egg yolks and cayenne. Mix well. Beat the egg whites until they are stiff. Pour the smoked salmon mixture into a bowl and fold in a little of the egg white. When the mixture has absorbed that amount, fold in the rest. Liberally butter a 1.5 litre (2½ pint) soufflé dish and tie a greaseproof collar around the top. Preheat the oven to 425°F/220°C Gas Mark 7 and pour the soufflé mixture into the dish. Scatter the cheese over the top. Bake in a hot oven for 20 minutes or until it has risen and is brown but the centre is still soft. Serve immediately.

Can be used as a substitute in:
Gratin of Scampi and Avocado, page 105
As a stuffing in globe artichokes and avocados
In Salmon and Spinach Parcels, pages 80–81
These sauces go particularly well with smoked salmon:
Mustard (page 171), Herb (page 171), Caper (page 173), Green Peppercorn (page 173) and Horseradish (page 174).

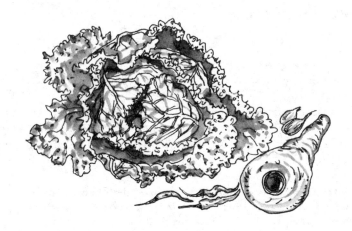

Smoked Sprats

Available in all smoked fish shops. They are cured like bloaters, placed in brine for a short while and then lightly smoked. They are very cheap and appear not to be particularly popular. The skin should not be dry and papery, they should be moist inside.

Smoked sprats can be eaten hot or cold. They can be lightly grilled and eaten with lemon juice and cayenne pepper. They can also be filleted, though they are so small that most people would think them not worth the trouble.

Smoked Trout

Widely available all the year round and probably one of the most popular of the smoked fish. More are now on the market than ever before because of the great number of farmed trout. Here again the quality varies greatly. And the look of the fish from the outside tells you nothing about the flavour within. Smoked trout should weigh between 100 and 175g (4 and 6 ounces), the flesh should be off white and come easily away from the bone. They're eaten cold with lemon and horseradish sauce; they make an excellent fish paste.

Smoked Trout Paste

3 smoked trout
juice and zest of 1 lemon
1 tablespoon horseradish sauce

150ml (5fl oz) sour cream
pinch of salt
freshly ground black pepper

Fillet the fish and put all the flesh into the blender jar. Add the rest of the ingredients and whiz until you get a smooth purée, about 1 minute. Refrigerate until you serve the paste, decorate with mint and eat with hot wholemeal toast.

Can be used as a substitute stuffing in avocados and globe artichokes, in mixed fish salads, puréed and added to smoked, layered terrines. The sauces for smoked salmon (page 123) are best for smoked trout.

CHAPTER VI

FISH FROM THE MEDITERRANEAN

3rd fisherman: . . . Master, I marvel how the fishes live in the sea.
1st fisherman: Why, as men do a-land – the great ones eat up the little ones.

Shakespeare, *Pericles*, II,i,26–9

Anchovies

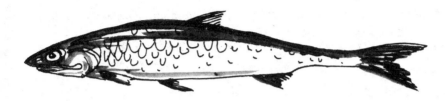

The anchovy is not a tiny sardine or pilchard, but a fish in its own right with the most distinct flavour. Hence it is of much use in the cooking of fish dishes. Fresh anchovies are found in markets in Spain and southern France and in the eastern parts of the Mediterranean as in Turkey where it is popular. In Spain they are called *boquerones*; the fresh fish are filleted and put in a marinade of oil, wine, lemon juice, salt and pepper. The marinade could not be simpler, they are eaten then as an appetizer and are mightily delicious. These marinated fish are often bottled and sometimes, but too rarely, imported into Britain.

Much of the anchovy catch is salted and canned in oil and this is what we think of as anchovies. But the fresh anchovy is another delight altogether. An even simpler Italian method is to marinate the anchovies, after splitting them down the middle and flattening them out, in lemon juice and leaving them for 24 hours. The juice tenderizes and cooks the fish.

The Turks clean and bone the little fish, flatten them out, then roll them in seasoned flour or corn meal; they are then deep fried and eaten as appetizers.

The Turks also cook the cleaned anchovies in oil, lemon juice, dill and parsley for about 8 minutes over a moderate flame. Then enjoy the dish when it has cooled.

Another Italian dish is to pour olive oil into the bottom of an oven dish, to cover the bottom with the cleaned anchovies, then sprinkle over chopped garlic, salt, pepper, oregano and parsley and finish with several chopped tomatoes. Pour a little more oil over and bake in a hot oven for about 15 minutes.

You can also treat the anchovies as whitebait, and simply flour them and fry in hot olive oil.

Salted anchovies must be soaked for half an hour before use. Canned anchovies are part of many recipes including the paste *anchoïade*. Patum Peperium (Gentlemen's Relish) is like a gentleman's version of this paste. Both are delicious, but *anchoïade* is rougher, stronger and cheaper.

Anchoïade

Blend two cans of anchovy fillets with a tablespoon of wine vinegar, 3 cloves of garlic, a chopped onion and 150ml (5fl oz) of olive oil, until you have a thick purée. Spread on French bread and bake in the oven until hot and sizzling.

Daurade and Dentex

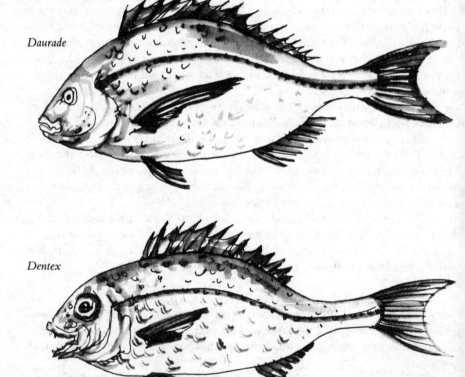

Daurade

Dentex

These are both members of the sea bream family but as they never leave the Mediterranean for the colder waters of the Atlantic (except for a few strays) there are no English names for them. But as they are both such magnificent fish it would be absurd to ignore them. They can sometimes be bought from fishermen in the UK. The dentex is the larger cousin, growing up to 1 metre (39 inches); the daurade never grows more than 60cm (24 inches) and can be baked whole in foil. But both fish are generally cut into steaks and fried or grilled, quite often served with anchovy butter. The daurade can also be cooked in a court-bouillon and left to cool, then eaten with salad and mayonnaise. Here is a recipe for a stuffed baked dentex which could be used for the daurade or any big fish.

Mediterranean Bream Stuffed and Baked

1 bream, about 40cm (16 inches) long	5 cloves garlic, chopped
3 tablespoons tarragon mustard	3 tablespoons olive oil
2 onions, chopped	150ml (¼pt) white wine
2 tomatoes, chopped	sea salt and black pepper

Lay the cleaned fish on a large piece of foil, slash the top and bottom diagonally across with 2 cuts. Paint these and the interior cavity with the mustard. Fill with the chopped onions, tomatoes and garlic, pour over the olive oil and the white wine. Close the foil, making a sealed package and place in a preheated oven at 350°F/180°C/Gas Mark 4 for 30 minutes. Take the fish out, open the package and baste it with the liquor, replace in the oven without resealing and bake for a further 15 minutes.

Can be substituted in:
Lotte Provençale, page 26
Roulade de Lotte, page 26
Baked Bass, pages 27–8
Marmite, page 31
Roast Eel with Apples and Cider, pages 36–7
Fish Simmered in Ginger and Soya Sauce, page 39
Flounder à la Deauvillaise, pages 41–2
Baked Grey Mullet, page 44
Stuffed Hake, pages 46–7
Flétan au Poivre, page 48
Dory in Cider and Cream, pages 51–2
Skate with Capers, page 62
Turbot with Crab Sauce, page 66
Many of the herb butters, mayonnaises and sauces in Chapter IX may be used.

Grouper

This is a very common fish in the Mediterranean and highly popular in the cuisines of Spain, France and Italy. Watch out for it on the menu, in Spanish *mero*, in French *mérou* and in Italian *cernia*. In Malta where I first came across this fish, it is similar to the Italian, *cerna*.

It can often be as much as 1 metre (39 inches) long and its width is about one third of its length, so it is a fat fish. Its flavour is very fine, with a dense white flesh, and steaks are cut for grilling or baking. Particular sauces have been associated with this fish and they work astonishingly well. I have cooked it with a sharp orange sauce made from blood oranges, and a blue cheese sauce made from Bresse Bleu. I have also cooked it *en croûte*, like swordfish, when you need a good 1.25 to 1.5kg (2½ to 3lb) chunk and it should be folded into the pastry with butter and chopped fennel. There are recipes from Turkey, Greece and Yugoslavia which all use various strong spices as in a recipe from Tunis which uses olives and salt pickles. It is a fish which is delicious cold as well as hot and one that could be treated like poached salmon if you ever get the chance of buying and cooking one of suitable size.

Grouper Baked in Blood Orange Sauce

4 steaks of grouper, about 2.5cm (1 inch) thick

4 blood oranges and 2 Seville oranges

sea salt and black pepper

25g (1oz) flour

50g (2oz) butter

Choose an oven dish large enough for the steaks to be laid out flat, and lightly butter it. Place the steaks in the dish, take off the zest and squeeze the oranges, pour the juice and zest over the fish. Season the dish and place in a preheated oven at 350°F/180°C/Gas Mark 4 for 20 minutes.

Melt the remaining butter in a pan, add the flour and make a roux. Take the fish out of the oven and pour the liquor into the roux, stir until you have a smooth sauce, then pour the sauce back over the fish and serve.

For other recipe suggestions see Daurade and Dentex.

Gurnard

You will no doubt see mounds of this fish in the markets, it is prettily rose coloured, like the red mullet, has spiny fins and large eyes. The head tends to be overlarge compared with the body, and you might not think it worth grilling, if not, it can be used in soups and is often an ingredient in bouillabaisse.

Monkfish, Angel Fish or Angel Shark

This is the fish confused with the angler fish (see pages 25–7) but this one is never seen in the fishmongers and is of no economic importance in the fishing industry for it is only caught accidentally. It lives on the sea bed and can grow up to 10 feet long. Smaller specimens do sometimes appear in Mediterranean markets and I am told that the flesh is good to eat. To increase the confusion between these two fish, the Spanish name is *angelotte*. Recipe books say use the flesh like lobster or scampi, but I cannot trust this statement as they are referring to the angler fish or *lotte*. I have never had the chance of eating this fish.

Octopus

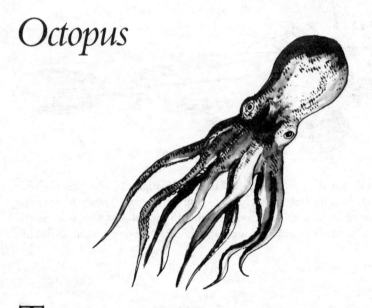

Though large octopuses exist they are hardly ever seen, and in the market you will only come across ones a little over 30 to 90cm (1 to 3 feet). This is *octopus vulgaris* which comes into the Atlantic and sometimes hits the southern coast of England, raiding the lobster pots. There are smaller octopuses, the curled octopus which is a distinctive and appealing shade of rust and *octopus macropus* which lives in the Mediterranean.

You are only likely to find these occasionally in specialist fishmongers in Britain, but you are sure to see them in any Mediterranean fish market.

To prepare, cut the muscles at the end of the tentacles which hold the contents of the head and turn the whole headpiece inside out; discard the contents with the beak and the eyes, then wash the interior of the head under running water. Beat the head on a stone for a few minutes to tenderize it, then cut the head and tentacles into strips and simmer them in stock or salted water for thirty minutes. Drain, and the flesh is ready for further cooking.

It can then be barbecued over charcoal, or made into brochettes with green peppers and tomatoes, then grilled or barbecued. Or fried in oil with garlic, tomato and parsley, or added to fish and tomato stews.

Stewed Octopus in Garlic and Tomato Sauce

One prepared and diced octopus
seasoned flour
4 tablespoons olive oil
4 chopped tomatoes, peeled and
    seeded

5 cloves of garlic, crushed
3 tablespoons tomato purée
sea salt and freshly ground black
    pepper
handful chopped parsley

Roll the pieces of octopus in the seasoned flour, and fry them in the olive oil in a pan, turning the pieces for a few minutes. Then add the tomatoes and garlic. Lower the heat and let it simmer for 25 minutes. Add the tomato purée and cook for a further five minutes. Check for seasoning. Add the chopped parsley and serve.

Mediterranean Prawn

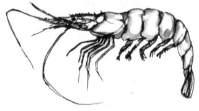

This is the most handsome creature and the biggest of the prawns, most often seen in restaurants hanging over the side of a bowl of chipped ice. They can reach 20 to 22cm (about 8 inches) in length. You can also buy them in fishmongers where they appear to be freshly boiled. But do ask. If they have been frozen and then thawed they will not be of the best quality. In Spain they refer to them as *langostino* which should not be confused with the French *langoustine* which is scampi. The French call this prawn *caramote* or *grosse crevette*, but I prefer the Tunisian name, *crevette royale*. In English they are sometimes called king prawns.

   To eat cold, simply snap the head off, peel the shell away and dip into a garlic or lemon mayonnaise. There are numerous ways to have them hot, there is the Spanish *Gambas a la Plancha*, where they are marinated in oil and lemon juice and seasoning then placed on a hot grill plate where they are basted every few moments and turned. They are cooked within ten minutes.

My own favourite recipe is a Portuguese one. This recipe remains a firm favourite with friends and family. I have never known it to fail to please. Using smaller prawns this recipe can work, but it is not nearly as good, though scampi or either of the lobsters are superb with this treatment. I once tried it with angler fish and that worked miraculously too. *Camarao no forno* it is called in Portugal, *Langostino al ajillo* in Spanish.

Baked Giant Prawns with Garlic

12 Mediterranean prawns
12 cloves of garlic, chopped
2 red chillis

olive oil
sea salt and freshly ground black
pepper

Peel the prawns and lay the tails in a shallow oven dish, squeeze the liquor in the heads out over the prawns (this adds immeasurably to the flavour). Sprinkle the prawns with the chopped garlic, pushing it down among them, then insert the chillis so that they too are snug. Then pour over enough olive oil to just cover the prawns. Season. Then bake in a hot oven 400°F/200°C/Gas Mark 6 for 10 to 15 minutes. Have plenty of fresh French bread ready to mop up all the oil and juices. Do not eat a red chilli. They should be avoided.

Red Mullet

A common fish in the Mediterranean. There are two different kinds and one of them, *Mullus Surmuletus* is a visitor to British shores in the summer months.

They are usually fried or grilled. On the Dalmatian coast, the fish are cut diagonally and the slashes filled with chopped garlic and parsley, then barbecued over fennel twigs.

They are often marinated in oil and lemon juice and then grilled. The fish has a delicious flavour and will respond to preparing in this way, rather than plain frying or grilling. It is a good fish to barbecue.

A French method is to bake the fish in foil with a strip of smoked pork or bacon, not unlike the recipe for Welsh trout, page 84. See also Red Mullet (page 58).

Red Mullet in Vine Leaves

4 red mullet
4 vine leaves
5 cloves chopped garlic

sea salt and freshly ground black
    pepper
olive oil

Clean the fish. Pour boiling water on the vine leaves and leave for a few minutes, drain and pat dry. Slash the fish diagonally across twice and fill the cracks with the chopped garlic. Season the fish liberally and lay each one on a vine leaf, sprinkle with oil and wrap the fish tightly. Place in an oven dish, head to tail. Sprinkle with more oil and bake in a preheated oven at 350°F/180°C/Gas Mark 4 for 20 minutes.

Sardines

Another fish which belongs to the Mediterranean as well as the Atlantic. The fish matures more slowly in the colder waters of the Atlantic which is why we have already dealt with them as pilchards in Chapter II. Fresh sardines are very numerous in the Mediterranean countries.

Fresh sardines have to be gutted and cleaned before cooking, they can then be grilled, fried or barbecued. The bigger sardines can be stuffed before being grilled. They are a strong tasting fish and an oily one, therefore they tend to deteriorate quickly so it is best to eat them the same day.

Fresh sardines can now be bought frozen in Britain. Freezing does not appear to destroy the flavour of the sardines as it does with so many other fish. They can be baked in the oven or cut up into slices and made into brochettes. They can also, like anchovies, be filleted and placed in a marinade for 24 hours and eaten raw in a salad.

Baked Sardines

12 sardines, cleaned and gutted
2 fennel roots
2 onions
25g (1oz) butter
sea salt and black pepper

juice and zest of 2 lemons
150ml (5fl oz) dry cider
generous bunch of parsley
generous bunch fennel leaves

Chop the fennel and the onions finely. Melt the butter in a pan and cook the vegetables for 5 minutes, then pour them into an oven dish. Lay the sardines alternately head to tail over the vegetables, season them, pour the lemon juice and sprinkle the zest over the fish with the cider. Bake in a preheated oven at 350°F/180°C/Gas Mark 4 for 20 minutes then sprinkle them with the chopped fresh parsley and fennel.

Squid

There is a common squid which lives in the north-east Atlantic, which also visits the waters around Britain. There are more varieties in the Mediterranean. Like the octopus you only find squid in the specialist British fishmongers, but there are plenty in the markets of the Mediterranean.

Squid is made for stuffing. After preparing it as for the octopus and saving the ink sac if you want to make a black sauce (see Spanish recipe below), stuff the head with herbs, breadcrumbs and the diced tentacles. This is the most common recipe. It can be excellent. It does rather depend on how tender the squid is. If it is small and the head is smaller than your hand then the chances are that it will be tender.

Squid can also be cooked as for the octopus. The most popular method in Italy is to dip the pieces in batter and to fry them. This very often can be a disaster, ending up with a plateful of india rubber encased in plastic tubing. If the squid or octopus is tender and the batter is a Japanese tempura, then the dish works.

Stuffed Squid

4 squid
3 large tomatoes, peeled and
  seeded
3 crushed cloves of garlic
3 tablespoons olive oil
1 tsp. oregano

1 tablespoon tarragon, chopped
1 tablespoon parsley, chopped
sea salt and black pepper
100g (4oz) breadcrumbs
50g (2oz) butter

Cook the tomatoes with the garlic and the diced tentacles in the olive oil for 10 minutes, pour into a bowl and add the rest of the ingredients except for the butter. Mix well and stuff the heads with the mixture. Melt the butter in an oven dish and roll the stuffed heads in the fat, cover with a lid and bake in a preheated oven at 350°F/180°C/Gas Mark 4 for 30 minutes.

Or try this Spanish recipe which uses the ink sacs. It is a great delicacy in Spain and can be a revelation. It makes a tempting first course, but you could eat it with rice as a main course.

Calamares en su tinte

900g (2lb) small squid, prepared
  and cleaned
150ml (¼pt) olive oil
2 large onions, sliced
5 cloves garlic, crushed
225g (8oz) tomatoes, skinned and
  seeded

300ml (½pt) dry white wine
sea salt and freshly ground black
  pepper
handful of finely chopped parsley
½ cup of beurre manié (see
  Glossary, page 195)

When preparing the squid take care not to break the ink sacs. Remove them and reserve. (You may find that the sacs have already been damaged and the ink lost in which case you will have to proceed without it. The dish will be just as good but the sauce will be a tomato red instead of a rich black colour). Cut the squid heads and tentacles into 1cm (½ inch) pieces. Pour the oil into a casserole and over a low flame cook the onion, garlic and tomatoes for a few minutes, then add the chopped squid and continue to cook for a further few minutes. Dissolve the ink in the wine and add with the seasoning and parsley. Simmer for about 20 minutes, then add the *beurre manié* in small amounts until the sauce thickens. Serve at once.

Swordfish

The swordfish is found throughout the Mediterranean where you are most likely to see it in the markets. But it is also found in the Atlantic as far north as Norway and west to Newfoundland.

You can buy it frozen in the UK, but freezing tends to make the flesh tasteless. Buy it fresh or not at all.

It is one of the great fish of the world in all senses. It can grow to 4 metres (13 feet) which includes the sword, which takes up a third of its length, but most specimens you see are around 150cm (5 feet); the body at its widest is often about 30cm (12 inches) in diameter, so the steaks that are cut from it are immense.

It is a superb fish to cook, as it has the one bone in the back and no others, the flesh is white and delicate, yet full of flavour. The simplest method of cooking it is the best.

Swordfish steaks of about 1cm (½ inch) in width need grilling, with a little oil or butter on them, then eaten with lemon juice. They can dry out a little in the grilling, so they only need a few minutes. Allow them to change colour, going from a translucent off-white to a pure dense white. Any left-over scraps of fish make a superb paste by blending it with sour cream or oil and a little more lemon juice.

I have had excellent results from home-smoking swordfish steaks. In fact it is almost the best way of cooking them. The paste from the smoked fish is excellent.

I have also cooked a piece of swordfish as large as a leg of lamb in pastry with fennel and lemon. This is good hot but even better cold. You skin the portion and bone it, an easy task, then wrap it in puff pastry with plenty of butter and chopped herbs, season well and cook it in a medium to hot oven for 45 minutes.

Swordfish is smoked commercially in both Turkey and Portugal.

Swordfish steaks can be marinated for 4 to 5 hours and then barbecued over charcoal. They need very little cooking.

This recipe I have adjusted from Alexandre Dumas's one for sturgeon.

Swordfish with Croutons

450g (1lb) swordfish
seasoned flour
50g (2oz) butter
2 finely chopped onions

2 finely chopped shallots
1 glass red wine
1 tablespoon of capers
croutons fried in butter and garlic

Chop the swordfish flesh up into small squares and roll them in the seasoned flour. Melt the butter in a pan and cook the onions and shallots, add the swordfish pieces, fry on one side and then turn them over. Cook for about 4 minutes until they are just done, then add the red wine and bring to the boil. Add the capers and cook for a minute longer. Serve with the croutons scattered over the top.

Can be substituted in:
Lotte Provençale, page 26,
Roulade de Lotte, page 26,
Marmite, page 31,
Roast Eel with Apples and Cider, pages 36–7,
Flounder à la Deauvillaise, pages 41–2,
Roes with Green Peppercorns and Cream, page 50,
Dory in Cider and Cream, pages 51–2,
Turbot with Crab Sauce, page 66,
Truite-saumonée en Croûte, page 82,
Creamed Prawns with Rice, page 101,
Poached Scallops in White Wine, page 103,
Gratin of Scampi and Avocado, page 105,
Soufflé, page 123,
If plainly poached, many of the herb butters, mayonnaises and sauces in Chapter IX are suitable.

Tunny

Another of the great fish which also belong both to the Mediterranean and the north Atlantic. The tunny fishing industry is large for we all know how common tinned tuna is. But fresh tuna is another experience altogether. You often find it in Mediterranean countries and steaks are cut from the body in the same manner as swordfish. You can also occasionally find fresh tuna in specialist fishmongers in the UK and in those large emporiums for the affluent. It is often frozen too. I have never tried frozen tuna, but I suspect that freezing might not destroy the flavour as it does with other fish. This is because tuna is a strong tasting fish, it is also very bloody and looks like meat.

No fish cookery book ever tells you to wash tuna repeatedly under runing water, except a modest Maltese cookery book I found a few years ago. I find this process helps the flavour enormously. For the cold running water washes the blood away and lightens the flavour.

Tuna can be grilled with butter or oil, but tends to dry out. It is better to bake it in foil as a steak or a large portion like a piece of topside of beef. But cover it and enclose it in butter and herbs.

I think the best method with tuna is to casserole it with various vegetables, spices and flavours. It will happily respond to the strongest of flavours, absorb them and be all the better for them – garlic, tomato, paprika, thyme, aubergine, onion, cayenne pepper, green peppercorns, oregano, can all be added in judicious amounts and the tuna reigns supreme.

Casserole of Tuna

675g (1½lb) fresh tunny
seasoned flour
3 tablespoons olive oil
25g (1oz) butter
2 finely chopped green peppers
4 large tomatoes, skinned and
    deseeded
1 tsp. dried oregano

1 tsp. dried marjoram
2 tablespoons parsley
2 teaspoons paprika
1 glass red wine
1 glass of water
sea salt and freshly ground black
    pepper

Wash the tuna under running water for a few minutes until it gets lighter, going from dark red to beige. Then dry the fish and cut into chunks, roll it in the seasoned flour. Heat the oil and butter in a casserole dish and fry the fish in it for a moment, turning it in the oil and fat, then add the green peppers and the tomatoes, continue to cook for another 2 minutes, before adding the rest of the ingredients. Bring to simmering point and bake in a preheated oven at 350°F/180°C/Gas Mark 4 for 45 minutes.

Can be substituted in:
Lotte Provençale, page 26,
Roulade de Lotte, page 26,
Roast Eel with Apples and Cider, pages 36–7,
Dory in Cider and Cream, pages 51–2,
Truite-saumonée en Croûte, page 82,
Gratin of Scampi and Avocado, page 105,
Smoked Salmon Soufflé, page 123,
Kedgeree, pages 118–19,
Excellent in mixed fish salads, and will make any of the pastes to be used in layered fish mousses and terrines, pages 162–4.
If plainly poached, many of the herb butters, mayonnaises and sauces in Chapter IX are suitable.

CHAPTER VII

SOUPS, STEWS
AND
FISH PIES

'The waiter roars it through the hall:
"We don't give bread with one fish ball!" '

George Martin Lane,
'Lay of the lone fish ball' (1855).

Soups

Soups can start with the court-bouillon which has had the fish poached in it. If this is boiled and reduced to intensify the flavour it becomes a fish fumet. However, you need not begin with a court-bouillon at all but with a fish stock (*fond de poisson*). Most recipes for fish stock include the fish head, but take care to remove the gills or else the stock will become bitter. Boiling the stock will also cause bitterness and if you add the fish skin you will darken the colour.

Basic Fish Stock (Fumet de poisson)

900g (2lb) fish bones	2 bay leaves
50g (2oz) unsalted butter	1 tsp. black peppercorns
1 onion, coarsely chopped	1 tsp. salt
2 or 3 stalks of celery, coarsely chopped	peel from 1 lemon
	1.75l (3pt) water
1 bunch parsley stalks	300ml (½pt) dry white wine

Melt the butter in a large pan and add the fish bones, cook them for a few minutes, breaking them up with a wooden spoon; now add the vegetables, spices and lemon peel and cook for another few minutes before adding the water and lastly the wine. Bring slowly to the boil, skimming occasionally. Simmer for 30 minutes then strain the stock through a sieve.

All soups and stews will greatly benefit from this stock, but there are two useful short cuts, where you omit making the stock altogether, and use water flavoured with seasonings. You can now buy in Far Eastern and Chinese stores a bottle of fish sauce. This is highly concentrated, almost colourless and rich in vitamin B – 1 tablespoon to 600ml (1 pint) of water is sufficient. This is the nearest equivalent to the Ancient Romans' favourite condiment, liquamen.★ Tins of clam juice can also be useful as a foundation for soups.

★Liquamen was so popular in the ancient world that there were factories all over the Roman Empire sited at seaside towns to make and bottle the sauce. Factories existed at Pompeii, Leptis Magna, Antibes and at Bithynia. The sauce was made from a great catch of sprats, anchovies and mackerel with added salt. The fish was thoroughly mixed with the salt and then left in a large earthenware vessel in the sun to rot. It was stirred and sometimes old wine was added, then left for anything from three to eighteen months. Then the liquid was carefully drained from the remains of the fish. What you then had was a fermented salty liquor of all the fish juices. This sauce was sometimes made from shellfish, a highly refined and luxurious product.

You can now buy bouquet garni which have been specially made for fish dishes. This is a lazy way of getting a flavour but, for town dwellers who do not have a herb garden which grows dill, tarragon and fennel, it can only be a good thing.

Simple Fish Soup

1.75l (3pt) fish stock
3 egg yolks
50ml (2fl oz) brandy

croutons
garlic mayonnaise (see page 169)

Simmer the stock, uncovered, and reduce by a third. Have the egg yolks in a basin, well beaten. Add a little of the stock to the egg yolks and mix well then pour them back into the pan with the rest of the stock and stir until it thickens. Add the brandy and pour the soup into individual bowls. Place the croutons and garlic mayonnaise on the table, each person adds a few croutons to the soup and spoons the mayonnaise over the croutons.

If you want a stock which will jelly for fish mousses it is necessary to use fish which are high in gelatin. These are: skate, eel, sole, brill, turbot, anglerfish, john dory, monkfish, dogfish, and any other edible fish of the shark family. For an excellent fish consommé, use the fish stock recipe above, but make sure the fish bones are from these fish. And use two tablespoons of olive oil in place of the butter for cooking the fish bones. When the stock has been sieved, place it in a bowl in the refrigerator where it will set. To serve, whisk the stock with a beater and pour over a little dry sherry, garnish with sour cream or mayonnaise. One of the best chilled soups for the summer months.

Two of the most famous of the fish soups, bouillabaisse and bourride are meals in themselves, where the fish is cooked in the stock and then served separately. In Britain we cannot make a classic bouillabaise as the Mediterranean fish, in particular the rascasse, are not available. However, we can make something like it.

Though the fish sauce made now in Far Eastern countries would be produced in a more sophisticated and hygienic way, it is still very much the same process. It is still the most favourite condiment in all these countries. In fact, so rich in B vitamins and protein is it, that a plain bowl of boiled rice with this sauce would be an adequate meal, if a dull one. The sauce is a necessary ingredient in most Far Eastern recipes for both fish and vegetables. It is also always on the table of the most modest café or restaurant. In Thailand it is called *Nam pla*.

Bouillabaisse

2.5kg (5lb) fresh fish (red mullet,
    anglerfish, conger eel, cod or
    whiting, scampi and mussels)
150ml (¼pt) olive oil
10 cloves garlic, chopped
2 onions, chopped
2 leeks, chopped
450g (1lb) tomatoes, peeled and
    chopped

2 fennel roots, chopped
2 dried red chillis
pinch of saffron
450g (1lb) potatoes, peeled and
    sliced
3l (5pt) water
croutons
bowl of garlic mayonnaise (see
    page 169)

Clean and prepare the fish. Leave the red mullet and the scampi whole and the mussels in their shells. Pour the oil into a large saucepan and put in all the chopped vegetables. Next add the red mullet and the rest of the fish. Add all the other ingredients and pour on the water. Bring to the boil and simmer for 20 minutes. Taste the soup and season it. Take out the fish and the vegetables and lay them on a platter. Pour the soup into a tureen. Serve separately with the croutons and the mayonnaise on the table.

Bourride

1.5kg (3lb) white fish (cod, hake,
    monkfish, whiting etc.)
50g (2oz) butter
450g (1lb) potatoes, sliced
450g (1lb) onions, chopped
2 leeks, chopped
5 cloves garlic, chopped

1.25l (2pt) fish stock
600ml (1pt) dry white wine
peel of 2 oranges
bouquet garni
sea salt and black pepper
croutons
bowl of rouille (see page 169)

Cut the cleaned and prepared fish into cubes, melt the butter in a large pan and add the fish and vegetables. Cook for a few moments before adding the stock and wine. Add the rest of the ingredients and simmer for 20 minutes. Stir well and if the soup is too thick add some water. Pour into a tureen and serve with the croutons and rouille on the table.

If a soup has the addition of flour and is further thickened with egg yolks and cream it is called a velouté. These can be made with any white or shell fish.

Dover Sole Velouté

675g (1½lb) Dover sole
50g (2oz) butter
50g (2oz) flour
1.5l (2½pt) fish stock
150ml (¼pt) dry white wine

2 egg yolks
150ml (¼pt) single cream
sea salt and black pepper
chopped parsley

Bone, fillet and skin the fish. Melt the butter in a pan and stir in the flour, cook over a low heat for a few minutes then slowly add the fish stock. Let it simmer for 5 minutes, add the wine, then chop the sole fillets into 2.5cm (1 inch) slices and poach them for another 5 minutes. Mix the egg yolks in a bowl with a little of the soup, stirring thoroughly, then return to the soup. Be careful that the soup does not boil but let it thicken slowly. Pour in the cream and simmer for another minute or two, taste and season. Serve in a tureen, garnished with chopped parsley.

Lotte Velouté

This is similar to above but chop the lotte (angler fish) into chunks and sauté them in the butter before adding the flour and fish stock.

Beautiful soups can be made from shellfish if the shells themselves are simmered in the stock, then pounded in the blender and sieved.

Brown Shrimp Soup

1.25l (2pt) brown shrimps
50g (2oz) butter
50g (2oz) flour
1.5l (2½pt) fish stock

75ml (3fl oz) sherry
2 egg yolks
150ml (¼pt) single cream
sea salt and black pepper

Peel ten or twelve shrimps and reserve them for garnish. Cook the rest of the shrimps in the shells in the butter for 2–3 minutes before adding the flour, cook for a further 2 minutes then add the fish stock and the sherry. Simmer for 5 minutes, then pour the soup into the blender, liquidize then pour through a sieve. Reheat carefully and add the eggs and cream as for the velouté above. Season to taste. Garnish with the reserved shrimps before serving.

Crab and Sweetcorn Soup

1 fresh crab
1.5l (2½pt) fish stock
50g (2oz) butter
26g (1oz) grated ginger root
275g (10oz) tinned or frozen
    sweetcorn

75ml (3fl oz) dry sherry
sea salt and black pepper
spring onions for garnish

Take the legs from the crab, break the shells of the two large claws, extract the meat and reserve it. Simmer the empty claws and the other legs in the fish stock for 5 minutes then pour the stock into the blender jar and liquidize. Sieve the stock carefully. Take out all the meat from the crab shell. Melt the butter in the pan, add the ginger root and sauté the meat for a few minutes. Pour in the stock, the sweetcorn and the sherry and cook for a further 3 minutes. Season the soup before serving it in a tureen garnished with the chopped spring onions.

Prawn and Red Pepper Soup

1.75l (3pt) prawns
1.75l (3pt) fish stock
2 red peppers
50g (2oz) butter

50g (2oz) flour
300ml (½pt) single cream
sea salt and black pepper
75ml (3fl oz) brandy

Peel the prawns and simmer the heads, shell and tails in the fish stock for 5 minutes. Place in the blender, liquidize and sieve. Core and seed the two peppers, chop them into small pieces. Melt the butter in a pan and sauté the peppers for a few minutes. Add the flour and continue to cook for a few minutes. Place two thirds of the peeled prawns into the blender jar and purée them. Add this to the red peppers and butter, stir and cook for a minute before adding the fish stock. Simmer for 10 minutes. Blend the soup briefly, return to the pan and stir in the cream. Bring back to simmering point, season, garnish with the remaining prawns and pour in the brandy.

Scallop and Mushroom Soup

6 scallops
50g (2oz) butter
225g (8oz) mushrooms
50g (2oz) flour

1.5l (2½pt) fish stock
300ml (½pt) single cream
sea salt and freshly ground black
pepper

Divide the coral from the white meat of the scallops, and cut each scallop into eight by slicing it across and then bisecting each slice twice. Wash the mushrooms and slice them thinly. Melt the butter in a pan and sauté the mushrooms until they are soft and are cooking in their own liquid. Toss the pieces of scallop and the coral in the flour and add them to the mushrooms, cook for 2 minutes then add the stock. Simmer for 5 minutes before adding the cream and seasoning.

Smoked Haddock Soup

675g (1½lb) smoked finnan
   haddock
50g (2oz) butter
50g (2oz) flour

1.5l (2½pt) fish stock
300ml (½pt) single cream
100g (4oz) grated gruyère
sea salt and black pepper

Skin and bone the fish and cut it up coarsely. Melt the butter in a pan and sauté the fish over a low heat for about 5 minutes. Add the flour and cook for a further 2 minutes. Pour in the stock and simmer for 5 minutes. Add the cream, stir in the gruyère and season to taste.

Moules Marinières

Moules Marinières is deservedly one of the most popular soups in the world, the mussel liquor flavours the soup and this first recipe is the classic one which is a triumph of simplicity. The second *moules* recipe stems from an Indian friend and is just as delicious but in another way.

3.6l (3 quarts) mussels
75ml (3fl oz) olive oil
3 finely chopped onions
3 finely chopped shallots
3 crushed cloves of garlic

300ml (½pt) dry white wine
50g (2oz) butter
handful of chopped parsley
sea salt and freshly ground black
    pepper

Heat the oil in a pan and put the onions, shallots and garlic into it, cook for a minute or two and then pour in the wine. Immediately add the cleaned mussels and put a lid on the saucepan. Simmer for 10 minutes, then take the mussels out and place in a large tureen. Throw away any which have not opened. To the liquor, add the butter and parsley and seasoning, simmer for a few minutes more. Taste and check the seasoning then pour the liquor over the mussels in the tureen.

Indian Moules Marinières

3.6l (3 quarts) of mussels
75ml (3fl oz) olive oil
2 finely chopped onions
2 finely chopped shallots
2 crushed cloves of garlic
1 dried red chilli
1 tablespoon garam masala

1 tablespoon tomato purée
300ml (½pt) dry cider
50g (2oz) butter
handful of chopped parsley
sea salt and freshly ground black
    pepper

Heat the oil in a pan and put the onions, shallots and garlic in it, with the red chilli and garam masala. Cook for a moment and then add the tomato purée and the cider. Bring to the boil, simmer and add the mussels. Place the lid on a saucepan and leave them over a very low heat for 10 minutes. Then follow the recipe above.

Stews

There is, on the face of it, little difference between some of the fish soups and stews; except that the stews have more varieties of fish and a thicker, enriched sauce. Fish stews are associated with Brittany, Normandy and the Loire provinces of France (a *Matelote de la Loire* made from eels, white wine and mushrooms has become a classic dish). Generally we cannot follow these classic fish stew recipes because the exact fish are not available, but what we can do is create our own fish stew combinations from what is available in the shops. Here are some suggestions.

White Fish Stew

675g (1½lb) of cod, hake and
  coley
225g (8oz) angler fish
600ml (1pt) prawns
50g (2oz) butter
225g (8oz) mushrooms
3 cloves garlic
50g (2oz) flour

1.5l (2½pt) fish stock
450g (1lb) potatoes
225g (8oz) fresh green peas
225g (8oz) carrots
2 bay leaves
300ml (½pt) dry cider
sea salt and freshly ground black
  pepper

Skin and bone all the fish. Peel the prawns. Simmer their shells, heads and tails in the fish stock for 5 minutes. Place in the blender, liquidize and sieve. Melt the butter in a large saucepan. Slice the mushrooms thinly and add these to the butter. Cut the fish into chunks and cook it in the butter for a few minutes with the garlic. Add the flour and cook for another few minutes. Now pour in the stock. Peel and slice the potatoes, pod the peas, slice the carrots thinly and add these with the bay leaves and cider. Simmer for 20 minutes or until the potatoes are just done. Season to taste. Add the prawns at the last moment.

Shellfish Stew

225g (8oz) scampi
600ml (1pt) prawns
2 crabs
1.5l (2½pt) fish stock
50g (2oz) butter
450g (1lb) potatoes

225g (½lb) carrots
900g (2lb) tomatoes
300ml (½pt) single cream
sea salt and black pepper
paprika for garnish

Peel all the scampi and prawns, pull the legs off the crab and remove the flesh from the claws. Reserve this flesh with the crab meat from the body. Simmer all of the shells in the fish stock for 5 minutes then liquidize and sieve. Melt the butter and add the peeled sliced potato and the sliced carrots and cook for a few moments, add the fish stock and simmer for 20 minutes. Place the tomatoes in a blender jar, liquidize and sieve. Pour the tomato liquid into the stew. Stir in the crab meat, scampi and prawns. Simmer for a further 5 minutes before stirring in the cream. Season to taste and sprinkle the surface of the soup with a little paprika.

Smoked Fish Stew

450g (1lb) smoked haddock
225g (8oz) fresh haddock
225g (8oz) conger eel
450g (1lb) potatoes
225g (8oz) small turnips
3 celery stalks
225g (8oz) leeks

50g (2oz) butter
50g (2oz) flour
1.5l (2½pt) fish stock
2 bay leaves
2 red chillis
sea salt and black pepper
handful of chopped parsley

Skin, bone and flake all the haddock. Take the skin from the eel and slice it thinly. Prepare the vegetables by peeling and slicing the potatoes, quartering the turnips and chopping the celery. Split the leeks down the centre, wash them and slice them thinly across. Melt the butter in a large saucepan and add the fish, cook for a few moments before adding the vegetables, stir for a moment or two longer and then add the flour. Cook for another moment but watch that it does not burn and then add the stock, bay leaves and red chillis. Simmer for 20 minutes, then take out the bay leaves and red chillis, season the stew and stir in a handful of chopped parsley before serving.

Fish Pies

Fish pies can be made from any mixture of white fish, with a topping of either mashed potatoes or pastry. The fish is chosen, lightly poached, then all the bones and skin are discarded (one should take great care over this, as finding either spoils the beauty of the pie). The fish is then laid into a pie dish, and a sauce is made and poured over it. The sauces can also be of various sorts, but a cheese sauce or a parsley sauce is the most common. The topping then goes onto the pie and it is baked in an oven for the required time, usually about thirty minutes, until the top is crisp and brown.

A fish pie is an economical meal, it is easy to make and tastes superb. The frozen ones that you can purchase are a travesty of the real thing; made just for two people and barely containing three mouthfuls each, they taste mostly of monosodium glutamate. Give them a miss and buy two or three pieces of assorted fish to make your own. Here is one simple recipe and several variations which become more and more luxurious. Once you add shellfish, prawns, mussels or scallops, you have a pie that looks and tastes magnificent.

Sea Fish Pie

900g (2lb) mixture of cod, hake
and dogfish
2 bay leaves
300ml (½pt) milk
sea salt and black pepper
675g (1½lb) potatoes

75g (3oz) butter
2 hard-boiled eggs, shelled
1 tablespoon chopped tarragon
25g (1oz) flour
50g (2oz) gruyère
25g (1oz) parmesan

Lay the fish in a large oven dish with the bay leaves and pour the milk over it; season the dish and place in a low oven at 325°F/170°C/Gas Mark 3 for 20 to 30 minutes. In the meanwhile peel and boil the potatoes, mash them to a purée adding 2oz (50g) of butter. Butter a deep pie dish. When the fish is cool enough to handle discard all the skin and bones and flake the fish into the pie dish. Slice the hard-boiled eggs, insert these amongst the fish and sprinkle with the chopped tarragon. Melt the remaining butter in a pan and add the flour making a roux, and cook for a minute or two, then add the milk which the fish was cooked in. Stir to get a smooth sauce, then add the two cheeses. When the cheese has melted, taste the sauce and check for seasoning, then pour it over the fish in the pie dish. Leave it for a while to allow the sauce to sink down through the fish, then spread the mashed potatoes evenly on the top. Bake in a preheated oven at 400°F/200°C/Gas Mark 6 for 20 to 30 minutes until the top is crisp and slightly brown.

Instead of the grated cheese a generous handful of chopped parsley could be added.

Smoked Fish Pie

450g (1lb) smoked haddock	25g (1oz) flour
450g (1lb) fresh haddock	300ml (½pt) single cream
600ml (1pt) mussels	sea salt and black pepper
50g (2oz) butter	a good bunch of chopped parsley
3 shallots or 2 onions	75g (3oz) wholemeal pastry
150ml (5fl oz) dry sherry	1 egg, beaten, for glaze

Melt the butter in a pan and add the chopped shallots or onions. Lay the smoked haddock, skin side down, onto the onions, place the fresh haddock on top of that. Clean the mussels under running water as on page 97 and place them in their shells on top of the fish. Pour the dry sherry on top. Put the lid on the pan, and cook over a low heat for 10–12 minutes. Turn off the heat and leave to cool. Throw away the mussel shells; skin and bone the fish and reserve the flesh. Sprinkle the flour into the pan with the butter and juices and make a smooth paste, cook for a moment or two, and then add the single cream. Stir until you have a smooth sauce, taste and check for seasoning and then add the parsley. Flake the fish and put it into the pie dish mixing the smoked with the fresh. Insert the mussels among the fish and pour over the sauce. Roll out the pastry, fit it over the top of the pie dish, and glaze with a beaten egg. Bake in a preheated oven at 400°F/200°C/Gas Mark 6 for 40 to 45 minutes or until the pastry is crisp and brown.

Fish Timbale

225g (8oz) cod	1 tablespoon curry powder
sea salt and black pepper	100g (4oz) mushrooms
75g (3oz) butter	225g (8oz) puff pastry
1 onion, sliced	Melted butter for glaze
200g (7oz) long grain rice	

Chop the cod fillet coarsely and place it in a saucepan with 1 cupful of water and a little salt and pepper. Simmer the fish for 4–5 minutes until it is just done. Take the fish out of the water and reserve both. Melt 50g (2oz) of butter in a pan and cook the onion, pour in the rice and curry powder. Cook for a moment before adding the fish water, put the lid on the pan, and let the rice simmer for 10 minutes. In another pan melt the remaining 25g (1oz) of butter, add the sliced mushrooms and cook for a few minutes until the mushrooms are soft. Mix the mushrooms with the fish and both with the rice. Roll out the puff pastry. Choose an ovenproof bowl big enough to hold the mixture. Line the bowl with three-quarters of the pastry, fill the dish with the rice and fish mixture and cover the top by turning in the pastry which has overlaped the sides. Roll out the last piece of pastry, shape it into a circle and place that over the top of the bowl. Brush with melted butter and place on a baking sheet in a preheated oven at 400°F/200°C/Gas Mark 6 for 35 minutes. Take from the oven and turn it out onto an ovenproof serving plate. Replace in the oven for 10 to 15 minutes or until the pastry has become golden brown.

Shellfish Pie

600ml (1pt) prawns
4–6 large king prawns
225g (8oz) cod, coley or whiting
600ml (1pt) mussels
4 scallops
100g (4oz) butter

50g (2oz) flour
150ml (5fl oz) dry white wine
300ml (½pt) single cream
675g (1½lb) potatoes
sea salt and black pepper

Head, tail and peel the prawns, put all of the discarded shells into a saucepan with 300ml (½ pint) of water, place the cod on top of the shells and add the cleaned mussels and the scallops. Bring to the boil and simmer for 5 minutes, turn off the heat and leave to cool. Take the coral from the scallops and slice each scallop down the centre, then quarter each piece. Take the mussels from their shells and discard the shells. Strain the liquor from the prawn shells and discard those. Reserve the cod. Melt 50g (2oz) of butter in a pan and add the flour to make a roux, cook for a moment or two before adding the fish liquor and the wine. Cook for a few minutes to reduce the sauce, then add the cream. Stir until you have a smooth consistency. Meanwhile peel and boil the potatoes and when they are cooked, drain them well and mash them to a purée with the remaining butter, season the potatoes and check and season the sauce. Butter a pie dish, flake the cod into it and place the prawns and mussels on the cod. Chop the large king prawns into several pieces, place these with the scallops and the coral on top of the pie, pour in the sauce and leave it time to run to the bottom. Cover the pie with the mashed potatoes and bake in a preheated oven at 400°F/200°C/Gas Mark 6 for about 40 minutes or until the top is crisp and brown.

A sensationally delicious pie.

CHAPTER VIII

PASTES, PÂTÉS, TERRINES AND MOUSSES

'Marry, sir, 'tis an ill cook that cannot lick his own fingers . . .'

Shakespeare, *Romeo and Juliet* IV.ii.6

Pastes

The crab or salmon paste found in a jar on the supermarket shelf is a dismal food compared to what could be made at home. Pastes are simple and economical to make. They will keep in a sealed jar in the refrigerator for months. They are well worth making.

In essence they are fish butters. They can be made from any smoked fish and from any strongly flavoured oily fish. Fish butters made from delicately flavoured white fish are not a success, for they are not pungent enough in flavour. The smoked fish does not have to be cooked but can be mixed with the other ingredients raw. The oily fish do have to be cooked first. The smoked fish that can be used are: smoked mackerel, smoked salmon (use the offcuts), oak-dyed kippers, smoked eel and trout. The fish that must be cooked first are: fresh herrings, mackerel, sardines, sprats and pilchards.

A quick, poor man's substitute for these can be made with tinned fish: tunny, salmon, pilchards and sardines. Drain the canned fish, add half the amount of fish in butter and flavour with salt, lemon juice, cayenne and black pepper. If making a fish paste from canned fish other flavourings are often desirable, a hint of any of the following would be useful: mustard, crushed garlic, soy sauce, Worcestershire sauce, Tabasco and curry powder. As you will see from the following two recipes the procedure is simple.

Smoked Salmon Paste

225g (8oz) smoked salmon
    offcuts
juice and zest of 1 lemon
1 pinch cayenne pepper

100g (4oz) softened butter
pinch sea salt and freshly ground
    black pepper

Place the smoked salmon bits into a blender jar and add the rest of the ingredients. Whiz until you have a smooth purée. It may take up to 2 minutes, but the smoother it is, the better it tastes and spreads.

Herring Paste

4 cleaned and gutted herrings
100g (4oz) butter
juice and zest of 1 lemon
1 tablespoon Moutarde de Meaux

1 tsp. sea salt
plenty of freshly ground black
  pepper
1 tsp. Worcestershire sauce

Wrap the herrings in foil and bake them in a preheated oven at 375°F/190°C/ Gas Mark 5 for 20 minutes. Turn the oven off and let the herrings cool. Carefully unwrap them, bone and skin them. Take the flesh and place in a blender jar with all the rest of the ingredients. Whiz to a smooth purée. Put the paste into a jar and refrigerate.

Pâtés

Fish pâtés are cooked in the oven, sometimes in a *bain marie*, are left to cool and are then unmoulded. They are generally sliced at table. They are smooth textured and can also be spread like the pastes. They can be made from white or smoked fish and from shellfish. They are not made from the more oily fish which tend to be more coarsely textured and would not slice as neatly.

Whatever fish you choose is minced or puréed with the addition of flavourings, spices, fish fumet, cream and sometimes eggs. The procedure is simple and is true for whatever fish you choose. Here are two recipes.

Crab Pâté

Meat from 3 crabs
50g (2oz) butter
50g (2oz) flour
300ml (½pt) single cream

150ml (5fl oz) dry sherry
2 eggs
sea salt and white pepper
1 tsp. paprika

Put the white and brown crab meats in separate bowls. Make a roux with the butter and the flour, add the cream and the sherry to make a thick sauce. Add a beaten egg to each bowl of crab meat and season both with sea salt, white pepper and paprika. Divide the sauce between the bowls and mix well. Put each one into the blender jar and liquidize to a thick purée. Liberally butter a terrine dish or bread tin and pour half of the white meat purée into the bottom of the dish, then pour all of the brown meat purée on top of that. Conclude by pouring the rest of the white purée into the dish. Cover with buttered paper, place in a baking tin half full of water and put into a preheated oven at 400°F/200°C/Gas Mark 6 for 50 minutes. Test that the pâté is done by sticking a knife in the middle and seeing if it comes out clean. Take the pâté out, let it cool and unmould onto a platter.

Sole Pâté

675g (1½lb) Dover sole fillets
6 large spinach leaves
300ml (½pt) single cream
50g (2oz) butter

50g (2oz) flour
1 tablespoon green peppercorns
sea salt and black pepper

Ask for the fish heads and skeletons when the fishmonger fillets them. Lay these at the bottom of a pan and cover with water. Simmer for 15 minutes. Lay the fillets on top of the bones and simmer for another 5 minutes. Take out the fillets and place in a blender, drain 300ml (½ pint) of the fish stock from the bones and add it to the fillets. Meanwhile blanch the spinach leaves for a minute then drain well. Liquidize the fish and add the cream. Melt the butter in a pan and make a roux, add the fish purée to the roux and make a thick sauce. Sprinkle in the green peppercorns and season with the sea salt and black pepper. Liberally butter a terrine dish or bread tin and lay the spinach leaves in the tin so that they cover the bottom and sides. Pour in the fish purée then fold over the ends of the spinach leaves. Cover with buttered paper and place in a *bain marie* in the oven as for the above recipe.

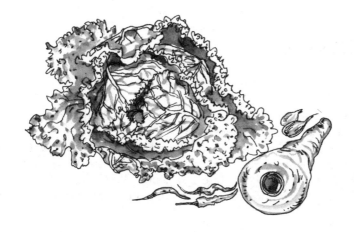

Terrines

A terrine differs from a pâté in that it is not only coarser but it has chunks of fish in it and is quite often cooked so that an attractive pattern is shown when it is sliced. Otherwise the procedure of making it is similar to pâtés.

Brill and Crab Terrine

meat from 2 crabs	50g (2oz) flour
450g (1lb) brill	300ml (½pt) single cream
225g (8oz) prawns	75ml (3fl oz) brandy
50g (2oz) butter	sea salt and black pepper

Keep the brill heads and skeleton and cook these like the sole above. Separate the white and brown meats of the crab and season both. Make a roux from the butter and the flour and add half a pint of the liquor from the brill and then the cream and brandy. Liberally butter a terrine dish or bread tin and cover the bottom with some of the shelled prawns, dribble a little of the sauce over them, chop the brill coarsely and scatter half of that over the prawns, cover with the sauce. Next put some of the brown crab meat in and cover that with the sauce and then the white meat and continue in layers until all the fish has been used. Cover with the sauce and more prawns. Bake as for the fish pâté recipes.

Mousses

Mousses are best made from smoked fish or shellfish. They can be delicate and delicious and make an excellent first course either made in individual ramekins or in one large dish. Do not, however, take the easy way out and use packet gelatine or aspic jelly. Make your own jellied stock from those fish that are naturally high in gelatin. Use 150–300ml (¼–½ pint) of this fish fumet with stiffened egg whites and cream. Fish mousses are extremely easy to make.

Smoked Fish Mousse

900g (2lb) smoked haddock
450g (1lb) fish scraps of skate,
  eel, sole, brill or dogfish
50g (2oz) butter

300ml (½pt) single cream
2 eggs
2 extra egg whites
sea salt and black pepper

Pour 300ml (½ pint) water over the fish bones and scraps and simmer them for 20 minutes. Steam the smoked haddock over the bones for the last 5 minutes. Take the smoked haddock flesh from the skin and bones and place it in a blender jar. Add the liquid from the bones and then the butter and cream. Separate the whites from the two eggs and add the egg yolks to the blender jar; season well, liquidize, then pour the contents into a mixing bowl. Whip the 4 egg whites until they are stiff then fold them into the haddock purée. Either pour into individual ramekins or keep in one bowl, refrigerate for several hours and serve garnished with parsley.

Layered Fish Mousse (1)

1.25g (2½lb) mixed white fish
  high in gelatin (brill, sole,
  angler fish, rock fish, rock eel
  or flounder)
1 carrot
1 onion
2 sticks of celery, chopped
juice and zest of 1 lemon
generous handful of chopped
  parsley

2 garlic cloves
2 tablespoons freshly chopped
  tarragon
225g (8oz) ricotta cheese
1 tin laver
½ tsp. powered coriander
1 tsp. paprika
sea salt and freshly ground black
  pepper

Have the fishmonger fillet the fish but ensure that you keep all the heads and bones. Place the heads and bones in a saucepan with the carrot, onion, celery, juice and zest of lemon and garlic cloves, and cover with cold water. Bring to the boil and simmer for 15 minutes. Lay the filleted fish gently on top of the bones. Simmer for a further 5 minutes or until the fish is just cooked. Leave to cool, take the fish out and place in a blender jar or food processor. Add the chopped parsley and tarragon and the ricotta and blend to a purée. In another bowl, tip out the contents of the tin of laver, add the coriander and paprika and mash to a purée. Season both purées with the salt and pepper to taste. Pour off the fish stock from the bones and add 150ml (¼ pint) of it to the laver. Add

300ml (½ pint) to the white fish purée. Take out half of the white fish purée and reserve for the spinach moulds below. In a soufflé dish or glass mould, place some of the white fish purée, then add a layer of the laver purée and continue in stripes of black and white until you have used up all the purée. Refrigerate for 3 hours.

Layered Fish Mousse (2)

Instead of the laver use a mushroom purée. Cook 450g (1lb) of mushrooms with 25g (1oz) of butter in a pan until they are soft. Season with salt and pepper and the coriander and paprika, then blend to a thick purée in a food processor. Add some of the fish stock as for above and continue.

Fish and Spinach Moulds

10 spinach leaves
the white fish purée from above
2 beaten eggs

150ml (¼pt) single cream
butter

This dish is made in individual ramekins or small moulds. Blanch the spinach leaves in boiling water for 1 minute and drain by hanging over the side of a colander. Cut out any fibrous stalk. Butter the individual ramekins and lay each leaf at the bottom of the ramekin and allow it to come up the sides leaving enough at the top to fold over. This task must be a little like dressmaking as you have to cut and shape the leaves to fit the moulds. Beat the eggs and cream into the purée. Spoon in enough purée to reach two-thirds of the way up the ramekin and fold over the spinach leaf or leaves so that the purée is enclosed. Place each ramekin into a baking tin filled with hot water so that they are standing in a water bath or *bain marie*. Place a small knob of butter on top of each mould and bake in a preheated oven at 400°F/200°C/Gas Mark 6 for 25 to 30 minutes or until the top of the mould has risen slightly. Take from the oven and allow the moulds to rest for 5 minutes before turning them out.

CHAPTER IX

HERB BUTTERS, MAYONNAISES AND SAUCES

Here capers grace a sauce vermilion
Whose fragrant odours to the soul are blown.
Here pungent garlic meets the eager sight
And whets with savour sharp the appetite,
While olives turn to shadowed night the day,
And salted fish in slices rims the tray . . .

Ibn al-Mu'tazz,
'A tray of hors d'oeuvre at the Calif's banquet'

Herb Butters

The simplest accompaniment to most fish is a round of butter that has been flavoured with herbs or spices. The most famous one is called *Maître d'Hotel* and crops up in menus all over the world. We know it as parsley butter. Here is the recipe because all the other butters follow the same principle.

PARSLEY BUTTER have 100g (4oz) of softened butter in a bowl, add a good handful of finely chopped parsley to it and a squeeze of lemon juice and some freshly ground black pepper. Mix well. Place the butter at one end of a piece of greaseproof paper, roll it up and place in the deep freeze. Whenever you want butter to garnish fish you can cut a circle from the parsley butter.

Tarragon butter is made by the same method.

LEMON BUTTER Juice and zest of 1 lemon added to the same amount of butter with plenty of freshly ground black pepper. Follow the same method as above.

ANCHOVY BUTTER Add one tin of anchovies well drained and pounded to a purée to the same amount of butter and follow the method above.

CRAB BUTTER Add half of the brown meat of one crab to the same amount of butter with a teaspoon of lemon juice and a pinch of cayenne pepper.

GARLIC BUTTER Crush six cloves of garlic into the same amount of butter, add one tablespoon of finely chopped parsley and follow the same method above.

MUSTARD BUTTER Add one tablespoon of English mustard powder and one tablespoon of Moutarde de Meaux to the same amount of butter. Mix thoroughly and follow the same method as above.

SPICED BUTTER Add one tablespoon of curry powder, one tablespoon of garam masala, the juice and zest of one lemon and half a teaspoon of salt to the same amount of butter. Mix thoroughly and follow the method as above.

WATERCRESS BUTTER Place half a bunch of watercress in a food processor and reduce to a fine dry purée. Add this to the butter with a pinch of salt and freshly ground black pepper. Mix thoroughly and follow the method as above.

Mayonnaise

Mayonnaise is an emulsion of oil and vinegar or lemon stabilized with egg yolk. The first recipe is for a basic mayonnaise. Then there are variations on it. Home-made mayonnaise is infinitely better than any make you can buy in a jar. These are stabilized with chemicals and further additives to prolong their shelf life. Mayonnaise is simple to make if you master a few golden rules. It is also extremely fulfilling for there is something magical about egg yolk and oil being transformed into this smooth creamy sauce. Some people make mayonnaise in a blender and if it works well who am I to complain? I enjoy making mayonnaise with the old method.

The rules to remember are: eggs, oil and mixing bowl must never be chilled, they must always be at room temperature; use a large mixing bowl which is heavy enough not to move around on the table, a wooden spoon and a jug to hold the oil with which you can easily control how much oil is poured in. In Spain they sell special oil pourers for making mayonnaise. Some powdered English mustard will help the emulsion, this is the French method and some people disapprove of it. A few drops of vinegar or lemon juice help to acidify the yolks before you add the oil. Some people dislike the overpowering flavour of olive oil and will use half sunflower to half olive. A mayonnaise made completely from sunflower or corn oil is a feeble thing.

Each of us who love making mayonnaise use our own individual touches and methods which become a ritual. Here is the recipe that I am happiest with.

Mayonnaise

2 egg yolks
1 tsp. mustard powder
2 drops white wine vinegar
300ml (½pt) olive oil

1 tablespoon lemon juice
1 good pinch salt
freshly ground black pepper

In the bowl mix the egg yolks with the mustard powder and the wine vinegar so that they become a paste. Measure out the olive oil and pour it into a jug. Hold the jug of olive oil over the edge of the bowl and add the oil drop by drop, stirring it in quickly with a wooden spoon. Continue without pause, pouring and stirring, never add more oil until the last few drops have been amalgamated; as the sauce grows in bulk so the oil can be added in a steady thin stream. When all the oil has been amalgamated it should be very stiff sauce. Beat in the lemon juice which will lighten and bleach the mayonnaise then add the sea salt and the black pepper. If the sauce is still too thick beat in a little water, a teaspoon at a time but take care, a mayonnaise with these amounts of ingredients will absorb, at the most, two teaspoons of water.

AÏOLI (GARLIC MAYONNAISE) Make the mayonnaise as above, then after beating in the lemon juice add four crushed cloves of garlic. This is a marvellous mayonnaise with assorted cold fish or shellfish salads.

ROUILLE Pound and crush one fresh red chilli which has been seeded. The easiest method is to put it into a food processor and reduce it to pulp. Add this pulp with the same amount of garlic as the recipe above at the same time and also beat in one tablespoon of tomato purée.

REMOULADE Add to the mayonnaise above two heaped tablespoons of mixed capers, basil, tarragon, gherkin and parsley plus a tablespoon of Moutarde de Meaux and a teaspoon of anchovy essence. Mix thoroughly together.

GREEN MAYONNAISE Place two or three leaves of young spinach in a food processor with some sprigs of watercress, chives and chervil. Blend to a thick green paste and add this to the mayonnaise above.

MAYONNAISE ESCOFFIER To the aïoli recipe above add one tablespoonful each of the following: finely grated horseradish, finely chopped shallot and finely chopped parsley. Mix thoroughly together.

SAUCE TARTARE To the aïoli recipe above add one teaspoon each of the following: gherkins, shallots, green pepper, parsley, all finely chopped with 1 teaspoon each capers and green peppercorns.

Sauces

Many sauces derive from the plain white sauce that is called *sauce béchamel*. This basically is a butter, milk and flour sauce, simply seasoned. But the milk can be flavoured by being infused with onion, carrot, bay leaves, parsley and nutmeg. The sauce can also be enriched by using single cream and egg yolks, though both together would make a very heavy, overrich sauce. Most of the white sauces for fish will have had the liquor that the fish has cooked in added to it. Or quite often the milk which will make the sauce will have already been used in cooking the fish.

White Sauce

25g (1oz) butter
25g (1oz) flour
300ml (½pt) milk

pinch of nutmeg
sea salt and freshly ground black
  pepper

Melt the butter in a pan, add the flour and make a roux. Let it cook for a moment then add the milk and keep stirring so that it does not stick at the bottom and add the seasonings. Most recipes tell you to heat the milk first as this will help to avoid lumps in the sauce. This is not really necessary if you keep stirring the sauce.

CHEESE SAUCE (Sauce Mornay). To the white sauce above add 50g (2oz) grated gruyère, 25g (1oz) grated strong flavoured cheddar and 25g (1oz) grated parmesan. Mix it into the sauce over the flame until the cheeses have melted and you have a thick sauce.

CREAM SAUCE To the white sauce above add 150ml (¼ pint) double cream. Stir the sauce until it is thick and smooth.

CRAB SAUCE Place the milk into a blender and add all the flesh from one crab. Liquidize and add this crab milk to the roux in the pan in the normal way above.

ANCHOVY SAUCE Drain the fillets from the tin of anchovies and place in a blender jar with the milk. Liquidize and add the anchovy milk to the roux in the pan.

MUSSEL SAUCE Open a dozen mussels and place them in the blender jar with their liquor and the milk. Liquidize and add this mussel milk to the roux.

CURRY SAUCE Make the white sauce above with 50g (2oz) of butter and add one tablespoon of curry powder to the butter, cooking for a moment before adding the flour. Then proceed in the above way but finish the sauce by adding 2 tablespoons of chopped fresh coriander.

MUSTARD SAUCE After making the white sauce above, add two tablespoons of Moutarde de Meaux, stirring it well into the sauce.

HERB SAUCE To the white sauce above add one tablespoon each of the following herbs, finely chopped: chives, chervil, mint, parsley, tarragon.

FENNEL SAUCE Have a good bunch of fennel leaves finely chopped and add it to the sauce. The green fennel looks better than the bronze.

Tomato Sauce

900g (2lb) tomatoes
4 crushed cloves garlic
150ml (5fl oz) dry sherry

1 bunch basil leaves
sea salt and black pepper

Cut the tomatoes in half and throw them into a saucepan with the rest of the ingredients. Place the pan over a very low heat, put a lid on it and forget about it for 10 minutes. The tomatoes will steam in their own juice. Turn off the heat and let the pan cool.

Pour the contents into a blender jar and liquidize. Sieve the liquor and discard all the bits of seed and skin. Reheat the tomato stock and reduce by a half.

Fennel Sauce

2 heads of fennel
300ml (½pt) fish fumet
150ml (¼pt) double cream

bunch of fennel leves
sea salt and black pepper

Chop the fennel heads coarsely after discarding the most fibrous parts. Simmer them in the fish fumet until they are tender, about 15 minutes. Let the pan cool then pour into a blender jar and liquidize to a purée. Reheat the sauce and add the double cream and chopped fennel leaves. Mix to a smooth sauce, check and taste for seasoning.

Shrimp Sauce

600ml (1pt) brown shrimps
300ml (½pt) fish fumet
150ml (5fl oz) dry sherry

pinch of cayenne pepper
2 tsp. tomato purée
150ml (¼pt) double cream

Simmer all the shrimps (in their shells) in the fish fumet for 10 minutes then pour into a blender jar, liquidize and sieve. Pour the shrimp stock back into the pan and reheat adding the sherry and the cayenne pepper and the tomato purée. Pour in the double cream and mix to a smooth sauce.

Crab and Brandy Sauce

Meat from 1 crab
300ml (½pt) fish fumet
75ml (3fl oz) brandy

sea salt and black pepper
150ml (¼pt) double cream

Pour the fish fumet into a blender jar and add the crab meat and brandy, season to taste and liquidize to smooth consistency. Pour into a pan, heat gently and add the cream.

Hollandaise Sauce

This is an emulsion of egg yolks and butter flavoured with vinegar and lemon juice.

3 egg yolks
1 tsp. white wine vinegar
½ tsp. white pepper

pinch of salt
100g (4oz) butter
juice and zest of 1 lemon

Place the egg yolks into a double saucepan and mix in the wine vinegar, the pepper and salt. Bring the water to the boil in the double boiler then let it simmer, chop the butter up into small pieces and add them to the egg yolks a piece at a time, stirring all the time. Do not add more butter until the previous piece has been absorbed. At the last moment beat in the lemon juice and zest. The sauce should be warm and eaten immediately.

MALTESE SAUCE Instead of the lemon juice and zest use the juice and zest of a blood orange.

Vinaigrette Sauces

These are sauces for fish which are derived from the basic vinaigrette that we use for green salads. They are particularly good with fish that are fried, grilled or barbecued.

Basic Sauce Vinaigrette

1 tablespoon red wine vinegar
1 clove garlic, crushed
1 good pinch of sea salt

freshly ground black pepper
4 tablespoons extra virgin olive
   oil

Pour the wine vinegar into a jug and add the garlic, salt and pepper. Stir thoroughly then add the oil slowly in a steady stream, beating all the time so that you have a creamy emulsion. To this sauce can be added an infinite number of variants.

CAPER SAUCE 1 tablespoon of capers added to the vinaigrette above.

GREEN PEPPERCORN SAUCE 1 tablespoon of green peppercorns and 2 table-spoons of sour cream beaten into the sauce vinaigrette above.

SPICED SAUCE 2 teaspoons of curry powder, ½ teaspoon Worcestershire sauce, ½ teaspoon soy sauce, 3 drops Tabasco, 2 teaspoons of honey and 1 tablespoon of sour cream beaten into the sauce vinaigrette above.

WALNUT SAUCE Use walnut oil instead of olive oil for the sauce vinaigrette then add 25g (1oz) of chopped walnuts and 1 teaspoon of honey to the sauce.

HOT PEPPER SAUCE Grind one dried red chilli with a mortar and pestle, add this to the vinaigrette with 1 tablespoon of Moutarde de Meaux and 1 teaspoon each of green and black peppercorns.

HORSERADISH SAUCE Add to the vinaigrette, 1 tablespoon of grated horseradish, 1 tablespoon of creamed horseradish and 1 tablespoon of sour cream.

TARRAGON SAUCE Use tarragon vinegar instead of red wine vinegar and add two tablespoons of finely chopped tarragon.

HOT TOMATO Peel and seed two tomatoes, chop them coarsely and add them to the vinaigrette, then beat in 1 tablespoon of tomato purée and 1 tablespoon of sour cream, add ½ teaspoon of Tabasco and 1 teaspoon of paprika. An excellent sauce with shellfish and simply poached white fish.

CHAPTER X

RAW FISH

'The fish in the river dart before you,
Your rays are in the midst of the sea.'

The Great Hymn to The Aten
Egypt, 1350 BC.

Eating fish raw has become more common over the last decade because of the popularity of Japanese restaurants. *Sashimi* is the name of the dish. But we do not really think of consuming fish from British waters in their raw state. Yet all fish can be excellent eaten raw. The Japanese in their *sashimi*, which is a raw fish salad, combine fish of different colours as they care for the aesthetics of the food. Three fish are nearly always used, salmon, tunny and sea bream. The pink of the salmon with the burnished oak colour of the tunny combined with the almost blue-white flesh of the bream is a delight to the eye. Salmon is certainly available to us and though expensive you need very little for this dish. We can also sometimes get tunny and there is no trouble in our waters in choosing a very white fish; both turbot and halibut would taste and look good. However, there are many more fish we could choose from.

Choose four or five different fillets. For a starter to a meal for 4–6 people 100g (4oz) each of salmon, Dover sole, smoked haddock, conger eel and turbot would be more than enough. Make sure that each piece of fish is fresh and choose the best part of it. Inspect it carefully and take out all the bones and skin. Place the pieces in a colander and pour boiling water over them, then immediately rinse them under the cold tap. Boiling water is not meant to cook the fish, but to kill any bacteria. Pat the pieces dry and slice them thinly. Cover the surface of either individual plates or a large platter with a mixture of salad leaves – two or three different kinds of lettuce, radicchio, chicory, sorrel, rocket – and lay the thin slices of raw fish in a pattern over the leaves. Squeeze a little lemon juice over them and serve them with several sauces.

The traditional two sauces which the Japanese use are *Wasabi*, which is Japanese horseradish, and *shoyu* or *tamari* which is high grade, fermented soy sauce. A sweet rice wine is sometimes also used as a dipping sauce. *Wasabi* is obtainable in small tins; it is a fine green powder, and you mix a little of it with some water to get a paste. Leave the paste for 10 minutes before you begin to use it. It is very, very hot and the heat does not come through until 10 minutes have elapsed. It is very good and a tiny particle of this paste mixed in with the soy sauce is all most people will be able to cope with. Both *tamari* and *shoyu* can now be bought in wholefood shops as well as delicatessens, Japanese and Chinese stores. As well as these a small dish of the fish sauce could also be served (see page 145) and if you have no *wasabi* the fish sauces could be mixed with green peppercorns or dry, pounded red chilli. The Japanese also grate raw ginger root into the sweet rice wine and this now is readily available.

We do not readily think of the more oily fish being eaten raw. But these too can be excellent. A fresh mackerel in peak condition, which has been carefully filleted, skinned and boned, and the fattest part sliced thinly, when dipped in one of these hot sauces, is a revelation in taste.

My advice is to be adventurous and experiment. If the fish is fresh, you are getting no loss of vitamins and minerals through the cooking processes, which is a point to remember.

CHAPTER XI

VEGETABLES AND SALADS

What wond'rous Life is this I lead!
Ripe Apples drop about my head;
The Luscious Clusters of the Vine
Upon my Mouth do crush their Wine;
The Nectarine and curious Peach,
Into my hands themselves do reach;
Stumbling on Melons, as I pass,
Insnar'd with Flow'rs, I fall on Grass.

Andrew Marvell, 'The Garden'

What do you actually eat with your fish? It is odd that some combinations of food are right and others seem to be a bad mistake. You do not serve carrots with cod, or turnips with Dover sole; yet a purée of mashed potato and some petit pois are suitable. Why? Is it just traditional? Are we just programmed to think that some food combinations are taboo? It is a difficult question to answer as food tastes are always on the move and new combinations suddenly become acceptable. This choice is also bound to be a personal one.

ARTICHOKES (GLOBE) When very small and fresh they can be trimmed and sliced into four, egg and breadcrumbed and fried in olive oil. One of the best vegetables which will go with almost any fish however it is cooked. If the artichokes are large they can be trimmed and boiled in salted water for 45 minutes. Let them cool then take out the centre leaves and the choke beneath, exposing the artichoke bottom. This will give you an artichoke cup that can be filled with a mixture of raw fish and shellfish tossed in a sauce, or one of the fish pâtés or mousses.

If caught short by unexpected guests, a tin of artichoke hearts or bottoms could be used. Fry them quickly in butter, squeeze lemon juice over them and sprinkle them with chopped parsley. The drawback is that the mineral salts in the can will still permeate the vegetable.

ASPARAGUS Another perfect vegetable to be used with fish. But because of the expense and its short season it is generally only used as a garnish. Fresh asparagus steamed briefly and then served in a salad of cold fish with aïoli mayonnaise is an early summer treat. A soup made from the scraps and ends of asparagus will make an excellent stock for a fish soup.

AUBERGINE Another good vegetable which can be used in several ways. A whole baked aubergine can be stuffed with fish or slices of the vegetables can be dipped in batter and fried.

Stuffed Baked Aubergine

2 medium sized aubergines
  (allow one half for each person)
450g (1lb) of firm white fish
  (Dover sole, halibut, angler
  fish, dogfish, john dory or
  turbot)
2 onions
2 tomatoes

25g (1oz) butter
3 tablespoons olive oil
1 tsp. crushed coriander
1 tsp. crushed cumin
sea salt and black pepper
good bunch chopped coriander
  leaves
wholemeal breadcrumbs

Cut the aubergines in half lengthways, place them face downwards on an oiled baking tray and put them in a preheated oven at 400°F/200°C/Gas Mark 6 for 20 minutes. Take them out and leave to cool.

Meanwhile trim and prepare the fish, chop the onions, peel and seed the tomatoes. Melt the butter and the oil in a frying pan and cook the onions with the ground coriander and the cumin until they are soft. Add the chopped tomatoes and cook for a few minutes more. Chop the fish into chunks and add these to the pan, turning them over in the sauce. With a sharp knife and a spoon cut and scoop out the flesh from the aubergines, leaving about 3mm (⅛ inch) adhering to the skin. Chop the flesh coarsely and add it to the pan with the fish. Mix thoroughly, taste and check for seasoning, add the chopped coriander leaves and pile the mixture into the aubergine skins. Sprinkle the top with a few wholemeal breadcrumbs and replace in the oven at the same temperature for another 20 minutes, or until the top is crisp and browning.

AVOCADO The avocado is mostly related to fishes as a receptacle for shrimps or prawns in *sauce aurore* which has come out of a bottle and is one of the most notoriously vile scandals of the catering trade. Add prawns to avocado by all means but toss them in one of the sauces on pages 170–74. But also experiment with other fish; crab, smoked salmon, smoked haddock and slivers of raw fish bound with a sauce can also be used to stuff avocados. This delicious fruit can also be used as part of mixed fish salads, stoned, peeled and sliced then lightly sprinkled with salt.

BATAVIAN ENDIVE These are becoming increasingly available in markets but they can also be grown quite easily in our gardens. They look like large, curly lettuces. Their centre a striking lemon yellow shading to a darker green on the outside. They are excellent as part of a green salad mixed with other leaves

But they are also sliced thinly, combined with diced apples, tossed in a mustard vinaigrette. Their slightly sharp flavour would be a perfect complement to most fish.

BEETROOT I am fond of beetroot, boiled and served hot with a white sauce but I don't think I would want to eat it with fish. But a raw grated beetroot salad in one of the vinaigrette dressings would be a good foil as one of the salads to accompany cold mixed seafood.

BROAD BEANS Fresh broad beans in parsley sauce to accompany a gently poached white fish would be perfection. But broad beans, boiled and tossed with butter will do. One of the very best vegetables for fish. Oddly enough frozen broad beans are one of the few vegetables when frozen that still retain much of their original flavour.

BROCCOLI Cut the flower heads from the stems. Slice the stems thinly and boil those in water while steaming the flowers above. Serve both together tossed in butter or in a white sauce.

CAULIFLOWER Cut the florets away from the main trunk of the cauliflower and boil them briefly for 3–4 minutes. Drain well. Toss in butter or serve in a white sauce. Cauliflower must never be overcooked. Alternatively, you could steam the florets, which would take about 10 minutes.

CELERY Celery hearts can be boiled or steamed. Alternatively the central stems can be chopped coarsely, boiled for a few minutes, well drained then tossed in butter with chopped apple and tomato. This combination makes a good hot side salad. Celery can also be used uncooked as an ingredient in many salads to accompany cold fish.

CELERIAC Peel the root and grate it into a bowl, blanch it for one minute then drain thoroughly and mix it with aïoli mayonnaise. This is an excellent complement to mixed fish salads. Celeriac also makes a beautiful purée for hot fish. Boil or steam the root after it has been cut into four, drain it well then liquidize with butter or sour cream.

COURGETTES Small ones can be steamed or lightly boiled whole and dressed with butter. Larger courgettes may be sliced and stir fried in a flavoured oil. They may also be dipped in batter and fried or dipped in flour and sesame seeds and fried.

CUCUMBER The classic complement to cold salmon. Slice a cucumber thinly, sprinkle salt over it and leave it for an hour. Wash under a cold running tap and dry, then toss in one of the vinaigrette sauces (cucumber salad). Alternatively a cucumber can be diced, salted, washed and drained then mixed with sour cream and mint (cucumber sauce – *jajiki*). Few people know the delight of hot cucumber which makes an excellent vegetable for fish. Slice a cucumber into 5cm (2 inch) chunks, bisect these then slice each piece into four. If the seeds are large scrape them away, plunge the cucumber lengths into boiling water and simmer for 10 minutes, drain well and stir in to the cucumber 2 tablespoons of sour cream and 2 of chopped parsley.

ENDIVE This is another good salad vegetable. It looks like a lemon green fright wig and often the outside leaves are damaged. This does not matter as it is the central part that is eaten. Cut the central corkscrew leaves away and add them to mixed green salads.

FENNEL Another classic foil for fish dishes. Cut any outside leaves away, trim the stalks and base and cut into four, steam or boil until just cooked through. If they're boiled, they will need five minutes; if steamed, ten to fifteen. Serve with butter or sour cream.

FLAGEOLET The most delicious and tender of the dried beans. Flageolet need no soaking before cooking but you might as well soak them for an hour as it cuts down the cooking time. If soaked they will need about 45 minutes simmering. Unsoaked they will take over an hour and consume a great deal of water. They are delicious cold mixed with any of the vinaigrette sauces. But they are splendid as a hot vegetable tossed with one of the herb butters.

FRENCH BEANS These are the pods picked young before the flageolet have grown. They are a delicious complement to all fish dishes and must never be overcooked. Trim the ends and either steam them for seven minutes or boil them for three.

LEEKS If leeks are boiled they easily become overcooked and unpleasant to eat. Here is the best method of cooking leeks. Cut away the coarse green leaves at the end. Trim the base and bisect the leek lengthways. Now you can clearly see where any dirt lies. Thoroughly wash the leeks under cold running water, then chop them across in 1cm (½ inch) slices. Melt 25g (1oz) of butter in a saucepan and throw in the leeks, sprinkle with a little salt and black pepper, put the lid on the pan and cook over a very low heat. After a minute or two give the pan a good shake and do so three or four times for the next eight minutes. The leeks should have steamed in their own juices with the help of the butter. In Dorothy Hartly's *Food in England* she gives a method of grilling trout by wrapping them in a leek leaf. These would be the wild brown trout which were smaller than the rainbow trout available to us now.

LETTUCE For a green salad use lettuce with crunch and flavour, Cos, Little Gem, Webbs Wonder and Iceberg. Try also to use a mixture of varieties in one salad; this is much more appealing to the eye and palate.

MANGE TOUT PEAS The mange tout pea has almost become a Nouvelle Cuisine cliché. We should not let this blind us to its charm. Pick them when very young, for if they are about 5cm (2 inches) long they will have some fibre in them. Boil or steam them very briefly. They will need 2–3 minutes boiling, 5–7 minutes steaming. Drain and serve with butter. There is another pea of which the pod can also be consumed and is similarly delicious – the sugar snap pea.

MUSHROOMS Another vegetable we associate with fish and it occurs as an ingredient of many stuffings. Small mushrooms can be sliced and fried in butter. Larger ones can be lightly oiled and then grilled or baked. If you are lucky enough to find field mushrooms they are infinitely better than the cultivated ones. Wild mushrooms are also excellent with fish: parasol, wood, ceps, chanterelle, oyster and puffball. Large mushrooms can also easily be barbecued or will be one of the vegetables, along with tomatoes and peppers *en brochette*.

ONION The family of onions, which includes shallot, spring onion and garlic is indispensible in fish cooking. It is, like the mushroom, a common ingredient in stuffings. It occurs in most marinades and in fish soups and stews. Spring onions are a necessary ingredient of salads and are added as a garnish; they're also used shaved very thinly in some vinaigrettes.

PEAS Fresh garden peas are a perfect complement to many poached white fish dishes. But because their season coincides with that of the wild salmon, when it is served hot they accompany the fish along with new potatoes. Try and pick, or buy, the peas when young, then they will only need 4–5 minutes boiling. The older, fatter peas of a paler hue, which have more carbohydrate in them, need up to 10 or 12 minutes boiling before they become tender. *Petits pois* are only available to us frozen or in tins. They are a useful standby.

PEPPERS Peppers can be used as an ingredient in fish stuffings. Their small cousin, the green or red chilli, whether fresh or dried, is frequently used for its intense heat-giving properties in many fish dishes, especially those recipes that stem from the Far East, Africa and the West Indies.

Jamaican Salt Fish Salad

450g (1lb) salt cod	1 cucumber, sliced
1 fresh green chilli	4 tomatoes
zest and juice of 2 limes	3 hard-boiled eggs
5 tablespoons olive oil	large bunch parsley, finely
freshly ground black pepper	chopped

Soak the fish in cold water for 24 hours. Cut the chilli open and remove the seeds, then slice it very thinly and put it in a bowl with the zest and juice of the limes, the olive oil and black pepper. Marinate it for as long as the fish is soaking. Drain the fish, take the skin and bones away from the flesh and flake the fish into a large bowl. Add the cucumber and the tomatoes cut into wedges, and the sliced hard-boiled eggs. Pour over the hot dressing and toss the salad. Add the chopped parsley and toss again.

POTATOES Potatoes, in all their different forms, accompany fish well. We all know the ubiquity of the chip potato.* But the deep fried chip is not a healthy food, we now realize, and I personally have always preferred the sauté potato which has a longer tradition in English cooking. The potatoes are peeled and boiled for about 15 minutes, they are then cut into slices and fried in butter and olive oil until they are crisp and brown. Mashing potatoes is another common method and potato purée, where cream and milk as well as butter are added, can also be delicious. The point to remember with both is to make certain the potatoes are cooked through and then to mash them vigorously; they should be smooth with no lumps. Do not put cooked potatoes in a food processor, for the energetic working of the blades breaks up the carbohydrate molecules and you will end up with a gluey grey substance. The taste is fine, but it looks unappetizing. Enjoy potatoes new if possible and boil or steam them with their skins on. Serve them with butter and chopped mint.

Another way of cooking potatoes to accompany fish is to use one of the French classic gratin recipes: dauphinoise, lyonnaise, savoyard.

Peel 450g (1lb) potatoes and slice them thinly with a mandolin or in a food processor, then soak them in cold water for 10 minutes. Pat them dry and lay them in a shallow oven dish with any of the following. Dauphinoise: pour 300ml (½ pint) of cream over, sprinkle with sea salt, black pepper and nutmeg. Lyonnaise: Slice 1 large onion thinly, interleave it with the slices of potato then follow the above recipe. Savoyard: Add 75g (3oz) of grated gruyére cheese, interleaving it with the potato, follow the above recipe. Bake all three gratins in a preheated oven at 350°F/180°C/Gas Mark 4 for 2 hours.

*Fried fish shops where fried cod and flat fish could be bought with a slice of bread and a baked potato began in the 1850s. The chipped potato was imported from France in the 1870s. This meal quickly became popular and was part of the staple diet of the poor.

PURSLANE A fleshy green vegetable which is delicious added to salads. It can be purchased in markets and also grown in our own gardens.

ROCKET Another green salad vegetable with a peppery taste that is marvellous in green salads. It can also be chopped and used in fish stuffings.

RUNNER BEANS The British rightly love this vegetable, but tend to overcook it. It should not be sliced thinly and diagonally for all the flavour is easily lost in the boiling. Top and tail the beans, then slice diagonally in 2.5cm (1 inch) chunks. Cook in boiling water for 4 minutes, or steam for 8 minutes.

SORREL This is a member of the spinach family and grows happily in the British climate. It tastes very strongly of gooseberries and is excellent made into a sauce for fish. It can also be a useful flavour in fish stuffings. Once sorrel is cooked it will reduce to hardly anything, but the flavour is so strong that very little will flavour a sauce.

Sorrel Sauce

225g (8oz) sorrel leaves   300ml (½pt) single cream
25g (1oz) butter   sea salt and black pepper
25g (1oz) flour

Strip the leaves from the stalks and put them in a pan with the butter. Put the lid on the pan and place over a very low heat. Leave for 5 minutes. The sorrel should have cooked in its own moisture and now have become almost a purée. Stir with a wooden spoon and add the flour, let the flour cook a little before adding the cream and seasoning, bring gently to the heat and continue to stir.

SPINACH Spinach, with its strong flavour, is another beautiful vegetable for most fish dishes. Cook the leaves without any water, but as in the sorrel recipe above, with a little butter and in a pan with a tightly fitting lid. The spinach should be cooked within 6 to 7 minutes and then need only be roughly chopped with a wooden spoon. Spinach leaves can also be used in another way as in the following recipe.

Spinach Fish Parcels

8 medium-sized spinach leaves
450g (1lb) raw white fish (cod,
  hake, haddock or whiting)
1 tsp. juniper berries
1 tablespoon each of the
  following, finely chopped:
  spring onions, shallots,
  parsley, mint and tarragon

175g (6oz) cooked, long-grain
  white rice
sea salt and black pepper
300ml (½pt) fish fumet

Cut the spinach leaves from the stalks and blanch them in boiling water for a minute. Drain the leaves and reserve. Put the juniper berries into a food processor and grind them to a powder. Take the skin and bones from the fish and place the flesh in the processor. Blend, so that the fish is well minced, scoop out into a mixing bowl and add the herbs, spring onions and rice. Mix thoroughly and season. Divide the mixture into eight and place each part onto a spinach leaf, roll up the leaf from the base, tucking in the sides as you go. Place the spinach parcels at the bottom of a saucepan, wedging them in so that they cannot move, pour over the fish fumet and simmer them over a low heat for 20 minutes. Excellent hot or cold.

SWISS CHARD A splendid vegetable. Both the stalk and the leaf are eaten, but they must be cooked for different lengths of time. The leaf resembles spinach and can be cooked in the same manner. The stalk should be simmered for 8–10 minutes, well drained and eaten with butter. One of the best ways of serving Swiss chard with fish recipes is to purée it. Cook the stalks for 6–7 minutes then add the leaves for a further 3–4 minutes. Drain them well and put everything into a food processor with 50g (2oz) of butter and seasoning, blend to a purée and reheat gently, adding, if you wish, a couple of tablespoons of double cream.

TOMATOES One can hardly imagine fish dishes before the discovery of the tomato. It has become the most common vegetable and flavouring with fish of all, saving only the lemon. As a vegetable it is grilled and can be barbecued or used en brochette. Large tomatoes can be stuffed with fish pâtés or mousses which are either eaten cold or briefly baked in the oven. It is added to fish soups and stews. It is the most common sauce with the salt cod dishes of Spain and Portugal. As a sauce it is a beautiful foil to poached or baked fish.

WATERCRESS Though watercress is useful as a garnish, its fresh peppery flavour is marvellous in a salad. It also makes an excellent herb butter and sauce. It should in my opinion be used with fish more frequently.

CHAPTER XII

SEA VEGETABLES

The man in the wilderness asked of me
How many strawberries grew in the sea.
I answered him as I thought good,
'As many as red herrings grow in the wood'.

Anon.

These are more generally known as seaweeds, but they have been renamed to give them a better image. They are an ancient food of man and in colder intemperate parts of our planet where populations exist near the sea they were a necessary part of the diet. There are many ways of treating them. In Greenland, Iceland, North America, Japan, the Shetlands and the Hebrides, varieties of sea vegetables are wind-dried in the summer and then used in the winter to enrich soups and stews. They are high in nutritional value, rich in iodine, potassium, iron, calcium and magnesium. Among their many vitamins they also contain B12 which, until lately, was thought not to exist in plant foods.

Sea vegetables can be collected from the shores of Britain, but as with shellfish take care that the beaches are far from any possible source of pollution. You will find carrageen, dulse and laver on coastal strips which are unspoilt, most particularly in Scotland, Wales and Ireland. Richard Mabey, in his invaluable book *Food for Free*, cites other vegetables and ways of preparing and cooking them all. Most of us will buy our sea vegetables from shops where they are dried and packaged. Remember that a small portion, once it is soaked, will expand quite alarmingly. They need very little soaking, about 10 minutes and all of them can be used, cut up finely, as an addition to soups and stews.

CARRAGEEN Carrageen is known also as Irish moss and it grows abundantly around the coasts of Ireland. It was famous in the nineteenth century as invalid food, being made into jellies and drinks. It is very rich in vitamin A, iodine and minerals. In the Second World War the people of the Channel Islands ate vast amounts of it and noticed that there was a marked decrease in colds and bronchitis. It will jelly easily and thus is good as an ingredient for cold jellied soups and fish mousses.

Soak 100g (4oz) of carrageen in 1.25l (2pt) of water for 10 minutes then simmer for another 30 minutes or until most of the carrageen has dissolved. Discard any scraps that are left and pour through a sieve. This will set and can be flavoured or added to stock.

DULSE One of the richest of the sea vegetables and one of the most popular foods, going back centuries. It has a long tradition in seafaring nations, used as a kind of chewing cud or tobacco. Scottish and Irish immigrants made it popular in the New World.

After soaking, it can be chopped and used in soups and stews but it can also be eaten as a salad. It will need slow simmering for an hour and then its liquor should be reduced to a few tablespoons which can be added to oil, lemon juice and seasoning. Mix into the salad raw mushrooms and a little onion.

KOMBU These are dark green strips which are rather like large bamboo leaves. After soaking they can be used to wrap vegetables or fish stuffings and then cooked like *dolmades*. Simmer the soaked *kombu* in water with a little added soya sauce. Soak for 15 minutes and simmer for the same amount of time.

These cooked strips of *kombu* can also be eaten cold if used to wrap leftover fish. Flake the fish, add herbs, seasoning and bind with either butter or a little sauce, then wrap pieces of *kombu* around an egg-sized piece of filling; tuck in the ends like a parcel and refrigerate for an hour. Slice across and serve as a salad.

LAVER Laver is gathered around the Welsh coasts and simmered in great vats for perhaps six hours or more. When it has become a black purée it is called laverbread. This purée can be bought in Welsh markets and lately it has been canned, and can be now purchased in delicatessens, or you can purchase by mail order from Mr C. Pressdee, Drangway Restaurant, 66 Wind Street, Swansea, West Glamorgan.

Laverbread is wholly delicious and can be used as an addition to fish terrines, where it will pattern the mould, or as a sauce with the addition of butter and the juice from a Seville orange. Because of its blackness it looks striking with salmon or any of the white fish. Like all the other seaweeds its mineral and vitamin values are very high. Traditionally laver sauce was eaten with mutton.

'A capital dinner! You don't get moor mutton, with hot laver sauce every day!'

Collins (1875)

NORI This is Japanese laver. It is extremely popular in Japan where it is the most common sea vegetable used. It comes in dried sheets which, once soaked, can be used in a variety of ways. The Japanese wrap rice balls with it and use it as *kombu* above to make little food parcels. Another common method is to use *nori* as a condiment. Lay the sheets under a grill and toast them, they will bubble and turn green. Crumble it in your fingers and sprinkle over the food.

WAKAME This comes in long curly strands with a centre vein which must be cut out and discarded. After the *wakame* has been soaked for an hour, slice it finely and add it to the salad. It can also be used added to soups and stews.

Kedgeree, page 118.

Smoked Fish Salad, page 121.

Baked Giant Prawns with Garlic, page 134.

Red Mullet in Vine Leaves, page 135.

Calamares en su Tinte, page 137.

Prawn and Red Pepper Soup, page 149, *and Scallop and Mushroom Soup*, page 150.

Shellfish Stew, page 153.

Brill and Crab Terrine, page 162.

POSTSCRIPT

No one could write a fish book today without stating a great debt of gratitude to that doyen of fish experts, Alan Davidson, and his two comprehensive books, *North Atlantic Seafood* and *Mediterranean Seafood*. No fish writer could ignore also that marvellous book by Jane Grigson which came out in the early 1970s – *Fish Cookery*. Nor could one ignore George Lassalle's *The Adventurous Fish Cook*. But over the years I have learnt more and continue to do so from the works of Elizabeth David. Her fish recipes appear throughout the famous books, garnered from travel, research and experience. You will find them in *Italian Food, Mediterranean Food, Summer Cooking* and in *French Provincial Cooking,* all published by Penguin.

GLOSSARY

BEURRE-MANIÉ Softened butter mixed with the same proportion of flour, used to thicken soups, stews and sauces.

BLANCH To plunge into boiling water for one minute then pour the water away and drain.

BOUQUET GARNI Can be bought as a packet of small sachets. Merely a contained mixture of herbs. Make your own by tying together sprigs of rosemary, fennel, tarragon, marjoram and chervil.

COURT-BOUILLON A stock of herbs, vegetables, wine, vinegar and spices in which to poach fish.

DEGLAZE To pour a liquor into the pan and to scrape away the glaze into the liquid as a preparation to making stock.

DUXELLE A method of cooking mushrooms which are used in stuffings. The mushrooms are cooked in butter or oil and then the flame is raised so that all the moisture in them is driven off, so they are dry.

EN PAPILLOTE means curl-paper and refers to the paper frill which decorates cutlets as well as the oiled paper parcel which wraps fish, enclosing it completely, which is then baked in the oven. Foil is now generally used for this method.

FISH CUTLET a thin slice cut across half or less of the width of the fish; it may include the centre bone.

FISH FILLET Slices of boned fish cut lengthways from the skeleton.

FISH FUMET The court-bouillon after fish has been poached in it, reduced to intensify flavour.

FISH STEAK A thick slice 2.5cm (1 inch) in depth cut across the entire width of the fish. It includes the centre bone.

FISH STOCK A stock made from fish bones and skin which when sieved and reduced also becomes a fish fumet.

GLAZE (i) The jelly over a cold fish; to glaze a fish is to paint it with a jellied fumet.

GLAZE (ii) The solidified juices at the bottom of a frying pan or baking tin caused by the fish, floured or not, being cooked in the fat.

MARINADE A liquid containing a mixture of wine, lemon juice and peel, vinegar, water, herbs and spices, salt and sugar; can also be used to pickle fish.

MARINATE To place the fish in a marinade.

MOUSSE A mousse is an uncooked pâté which has been lightened by beaten egg white and set by a fish fumet made from fish bones high in gelatin.

PÂTÉ Merely the French word for paste but we think of fish paste as something that comes out of a jar and can easily be spread. A fish pâté can be sliced and has been unmoulded from its cooking dish.

ROUX This is like the beurre manié, a butter and flour thickening agent but the butter is heated over a flame and the flour is cooked in it.

SEASONED BUTTER Butter with the addition of seasoned flour.

SEASONED FLOUR Flour with the additon of sea salt, freshly ground black pepper and possibly other spices referred to in the recipe.

FISHMONGERS

The Waitrose chain of supermarkets, and some branches of Sainsbury, have good ranges of fresh fish and knowledgeable staff who will prepare fish (e.g. fillet it) for you. Stalls at weekly markets, too, are often good sources of fresh fish, and in seaside towns and villages it is often possible to buy direct from local fishermen from stalls or huts on the beach.

England

Banstead
See Leach Bros, Coydon

Barking
Rainbow
29 Longbridge Road
Barking
Essex

Beverley
H. Peck & Son
7 Wednesday Market
Beverley
Humberside
HU17 0DG

Bexhill-on-Sea
Seafood Quality Fish & Poultry
71 Western Road
Bexhill-on-Sea
East Sussex

Birmingham
Don Perren
Swan Indoor Markct Centre
Yardley
Birmingham

G. M. Vincent Ltd
160 Alcester Road
Birmingham 13

Bishops Stortford
Taylors Ltd
(Specialists in Wet Fish)
6 Potters Street
Bishops Stortford
Herts

Braintree
R. L. Goodwin
L. G. Goodwin Ltd
Market Place
Braintree
Essex

Bristol
Tovey's Seafood Ltd
198–200 Stapleton Road
Bristol 5
Avon

Webb Brothers
Bristol Fish Market
St Nicholas Street
Bristol
Avon

Bromley
G. Cope
Widmore Road
Bromley
Kent

Bushey
J. A. Corney Ltd
47 Cold Harbour Lane
Bushey
Herts
WD2 3NU

Camberley
Robert Mackenzie
Fish & Game
22 Obelisk Way
Camberley
Surrey
GU15 3SD

Cheadle
Jack Bidwell
(Specialists in Scottish Fish)
39 Wilmslow Road
Cheadle SK8
Gt Manchester

Chichester
Hoopers Fresh Fish
19 South Street
Chichester
Sussex

Cley
Michael Rhodes
The Cley Smoke House
Cley-next-the-sea
Norfolk

Craster
L. Robson & Sons
Haven Hill
Craster
Northumbria

Cromer
R. & J. Davies
7 Garden Street
Cromer
Norfolk

Croydon
Leach Bros (Fishmongers) Ltd
25 Church Street
Croydon
Surrey
CR9 1EN

BRANCH:
105 High Street
Banstead
Surrey

Minch Distribution Ltd
97 South End
Croydon
Surrey

P. Rimington Ltd
111–113 Brighton Road
Croydon
Surrey
CR2 6YA

BRANCH:
26 High Street
Purley
Surrey

Rod White & Co.
319 Lower Addiscombe Road
Croydon
Surrey CR0 6RF

Derby
A. Roome
B. & A. Roome
43 Sadler Gate
Derby
DE1 3NQ

Durham
Ken Peacock
K. & J. Peacock
70 Saddler Street
Durham City
Co. Durham

Edenbridge
Edenbridge Fisheries
33 High Street
Edenbridge
Kent

Edgware
Nat Jacobs
7 The Promenade
Edgwarebury Lane
Edgware
Middlesex

Enfield
F. Berndes Ltd
see London

Fordingbridge
Brown's Fishmongers
High Street
Fordingbridge
Hampshire

Gerrards Cross
E. Bott Ltd
18 Packhorse Road
Gerrards Cross
Berks

Gillingham, Dorset
K. J. Richards
Signal Crayfish Suppliers
Riversdale Farm
Stour Provost
near Gillingham
Dorset

Gillingham, Kent
S. S. Morley
The Fisheries
129 Watling Street
Gillingham
Kent

Goodmayes
H. Cayless & Son
63 Goodmayes Road
Goodmayes
Essex
IG3 9UB

Grays
M. J. Candler
23 Orsett Road
Grays
Essex

Great Yarmouth
The Bloater Shop
66 Englands Lane
Gorleston
Great Yarmouth
Norfolk

Hartlepool
J. Fortune
Fish Quay
Hartlepool
North Yorkshire

Hastings
Hart & Son
52a High Street
Hastings
East Sussex

Henfield
Springs Smoked Salmon
Edburton
Henfield
West Sussex

Hereford
M. D. H. Gardiner
13 King Street
Hereford

Horley
Brian Bunkell
Bunkells
72 Victoria Road
Horley
Surrey
RH6 7PZ

Hounslow
John Masters
Peters (Market Fishmongers) Ltd
344 Bath Road
Hounslow
Middlesex

Huddersfield
J. M. Mansfield
H. Kilburn Ltd
18 The Arcade
New Market Hall
Huddersfield
West Yorkshire
HD1 2UJ

Ipswich
P. A. Capocci
296 Nacton Road
Ipswich
Suffolk

Kettering
John Mobbs
1–2 George Street
Kettering
Northants

Kidlington
Haymans Fisheries
29 High Street
Kidlington
Oxfordshire

Kingston-upon-Thames
A. H. Jarvis & Son Ltd
56 Coombe Road
Kingston-upon-Thames
Surrey

Littlehampton
J. Oxley
5 Surrey Street
Littlehampton
Sussex

London
Postal districts only

Arthur
18 Bute Street
South Kensington
SW7

Ashdown (Leadenhall) Ltd
23 Leadenhall Market
EC3

Berndes, F. Ltd
807 High Road
Tottenham
N17

BRANCHES:
192 Fore Street
N18

202 High Road, Ponders End
630 Hertford Road, Enfield
146 Lancaster Road, Enfield
55 Church Street, Enfield

Blackwell, F. A.
261 Well Street
Hackney
E9

Blagdon, John, Fishmongers
64–65 Paddington Street
Marylebone
W1

Boulters
Fish/Game Deliverers
53 Lavender Hill
SW11

Brookes Butchers, Poulterers &
Fishmongers
77 Bishops Bridge Road
W2

Chalmers & Gray
67 Notting Hill Gate
W11

Condon Fishmongers
363 Wandsworth Road
SW8

Covent Garden Fishmongers
37 Turnham Green Terrace
Chiswick
W4

Daniels, John
3–4 Myrtle Road
East Ham
E6

Gordon, Samuel, Ltd
76 Marchmont Street
Tavistock Square
WC1

Green, J. B. (Crouch End) Ltd
17 The Broadway
Crouch End
N8

BRANCH:
52 The Broadway
Muswell Hill
N10

Hamburger Products
15 Charlotte Place
W1

Harrods
Knightsbridge
SW1

Hatt, Steve
88–90 Essex Road
Islington
N1

Linwood, H. S. & Sons
25 Market Square
New Edmonton Green
N9

Mackenzie Bros (Smithfield) Ltd
508–518 Central Market
Smithfield
EC1

Minch Distribution Ltd
8 Shepherd Market
W1

BRANCHES:
23 Romilly Street, W1
97 South End, Croydon

Mist, Joe & Sons
254 Battersea Park Road
SW11

Portch, J. & Sons Ltd
378 High Road
Chiswick
W4

BRANCHES:
405 Kings Road
SW1

58 Northcote Road
SW11

379 Upper Richmond Road
SW14

Purkis, W. C.,
138 Hoe Street
E17

Richards (Soho) Ltd
11 Brewer Street
W1

Rowe, R. & Son (London) Ltd
242 West End Lane
NW6

BRANCHES:
11 High Street
NW10

554 Harrow Road
Paddington
W2

59 Broadway
W13

Saunders & Ralph
139 Pitshanger Lane
West Ealing
W5

Sea Harvest Fisheries
16 Warwick Way
Victoria
SW1

Selfridges Ltd
Oxford Street
W1

Stoller, Sam & Son Ltd
28 Temple Fortune Parade
Finchley Road
NW11

BRANCH:
8 Stamford Hill
N16

Treadwells
97 Chippenham Road
Paddington
W9

Vandersluis
6 Clifton Road
Maida Vale
W9

Wainwright and Daughter
95 Marylebone High St
W1

BRANCHES:
275 Kensington High Street
W8

359 Fulham Road
SW10

White, Bob
1 Kennington Lane
SE11

Loughton
K. C. Fisheries
1 Oakwood Hill
Loughton
Essex

Lowestoft
Raglan Smokehouse
Raglan Street
Lowestoft
Suffolk

Lyme Regis
Phil Bowditch
Fish Merchant
Rosemary
Whalley Lane
Uplyme
Lyme Regis
Dorset

Malvern
Fresh Fish & Game Supplies
78 Barnards Green Road
Malvern
Worcs

Manchester
Russells (Didsbury) Ltd
109 Lapwing Lane
Didsbury
Manchester 20

Marlow
Janet & Tony Storey
Shrimptons
23–25 High Street
Marlow
Bucks

Newbury
G. S. J. Thurgut
Newbury Fisheries
Shop 1
Inch's Yard
Market Street
Newbury
Berks

New Malden
John Demaine Ltd
"Scotts"
158 High Street
New Malden
Surrey

Orford
The Butley–Orford Oysterage
Market Hill
Orford
Suffolk

Peterborough
Bretton Fisheries
Rightwell Centre
Bretton
Peterborough
Northants

Ponders End
F. Berndes Ltd
see London

Portsmouth
Hoopers Fresh Fish
89 London Road
North End
Portsmouth
Hants

Purley
see Croydon
P. Rimington Ltd

Reading
Ron Eighteen & Sons Ltd
19–20 Union Street
Reading
Berks

Redhill
J. P. Basso
2 The Arcade
16 Station Road
Redhill
Surrey

Ryde
Dave Woracker
18 High Street
Ryde
Isle of Wight

St Albans
Warwicks Ltd
1 Catherine Street
St Albans
Herts

St Helens
J. M. L. Spaven
B. Spaven & Son
7 Barrow Street
St Helens
Merseyside
WA10 3RX

Selsey
Jeffrey Lawrence
Jeff Lawrence Fishmerchant
147 High Street
Selsey
Sussex
PO20 0QB

Southend
R. A. Byford & Sons
116 Eastwood Old Road
Southend
Essex

Southsea
Hoopers Fresh Fish
223 Albert Road
Southsea
Hampshire

Taunton
Phil Bowditch
Fish Merchant
Bath Place
Taunton
Devon

Teddington
J. B. Green (Crouch End) Ltd

BRANCHES:
J. Oxley
21 Broad Street
Teddington

Tunbridge Wells
Quality Fish
45 London Road
Southborough
Tunbridge Wells
Kent

Twickenham
James Brothers
56 King Street
Twickenham

Uppingham
Mr Patton's Pantry
High Street
Uppingham
Leicestershire

West Ewell
Jelley & Sons Ltd
208 Chessington Road
West Ewell
Surrey

West Mersea
D. & M. Mussett
Oyster Bar
96 Coast Road
West Mersea
Mersea Island
Essex

Woodbridge
Loaves & Fishes
52 The Thoroughfare
Woodbridge
Suffolk

Worthing
J. Oxley
10 Wallace Parade
Goring Road
Worthing
Sussex

Isle of Man

Douglas
John Curtis
10 Woodbourne Road
Douglas
Isle of Man

G. Devereau & Son Ltd
The Fish Centre
38 Strand Street
Douglas
Isle of Man

Peel
T. Moore & Sons Ltd
Mill Rod
Peel
Isle of Man

Wales

Cardiff
John Adams
E. Ashton (Fishmongers) Ltd
Central Market
Cardiff
Glamorgan
CF1 2AU

Llandudno
The Fish Market
Market Hall
Llandudno
Clwyd

Pembroke Dock
Pembroke Oyster Fishery
(Captain Cook)
The Delicatessen
Bush Street
Pembroke Dock
Dyfed

Swansea
Francis Greene
F. C. Greene Fishmonger
Swansea Market
Swansea
Glamorgan

Scotland

Aberdeen
Aberdeen Smoked Salmon Co.
52a Menzies Road
Aberdeen

Achiltibuie
The Smokehouse
Achiltibuie
by Ullapool
Ross-shire
Highlands
IV26 2YG

Alloa
The Fish Shop
Maple Centre
Drysdale Road
Alloa
Clackmannanshire

Annan
Pinney's Smokehouses Ltd
Newpark Farm
Brydekirk
Annan
Dumfries & Galloway

Arbroath
R. R. Spink & Son
24 Seagate
Arbroath
Tayside

Cairndow
Loch Fyne Oysters
Ardkinlas Estate
Cairndow
Argyll

Cairnryan
H. Wither
Oyster Tanks Cottage
Cairnryan
Dumfries & Galloway

Carsluith
A. E. Watson
The Galloway Smokehouse
Carsluith
Newton Stewart
Dumfries & Galloway

Dundee
Andrew Keracher
Unit 3
Keiller Centre
Dundee

Edinburgh
Campbells (Fish & Poultry)
18 Stafford Street
Edinburgh

Douglas C. Thomson
A. Thomson & Sons
104 St John's Road
Corstorphine
Edinburgh

Glasgow
Keith M. Cowan
7 Station Road
Milngavie
Glasgow
G62 6PB

Kirkcudbright
J. King
St Mary's Isle
Kirkcudbright
Kirkcudbrightshire

Longhope
John Steer
Crab Factory
Brims
Longhope
Orkney

Macduff
P. Porter
43 Church Street
Macduff
Grampian

Port William
J. G. Maxwell
93 Main Street
Port William
Dumfries & Galloway

Rothesay
Ritchie Brothers
37 Watergate
Rothesay
Bute

St Andrews
Andrew Keracher
108 Market Street
St Andrews

Northern Ireland

Carrickfergus
New Fish Shop
25 North Street
Carrickfergus
Co. Antrim

Londonderry
Armstrong Delicatessen
12 Bridge Street
Londonderry
Co. Londonderry

Port Stewart
Peter Nevin
The Promenade
Port Stewart
Co. Londonderry

The following are catering suppliers, selling mainly to the trade. They do, however, have show rooms and sell to the general public.

Birmingham
E. Coaney & Co.
Holloway Head
Birmingham

Luton
Roland Allan & Co
Harlock Corner
North Street
Luton

Leicester
Gerald Gamble
19–23 Amberstone Road
Leicester

Nottingham
Jessie Robinson (Nottingham) Ltd
12–14 Bath Street
Nottingham

EQUIPMENT STOCKISTS

Branches of Habitat, John Lewis and larger branches of Boots.

England

Bath
Kitchens (Catering Utensils) Ltd
4 Quiet Street
Bath

Bournemouth
Beales
Old Christchurch Road
Bournemouth

Bristol
Kitchens (Catering Utensils) Ltd
167 Whiteladies Road
Bristol

and

4 Waterloo Street
Clifton
Bristol

Cambridge
Eaden Lilley & Co. Ltd
Green Street
Cambridge

and

Market Street
Cambridge

Joshua Taylor & Co. Ltd
Sidney Street & Bridge Street
Cambridge

Canterbury
Elizabeth David Ltd
at: Nathans of Canterbury
High Street
Canterbury
Kent

Chester
Romani Kitchenware
Gods Providence House
Watergate Row
Chester

Harrogate
The Good Cook's Shop
16 Oxford Street
Harrogate

Leeds
Schofields (Yorkshire) Ltd
79 The Headrow
Leeds

London

Covent Garden Kitchen Supplies
3 North Row
The Market
Covent Garden
WC2

Dare, Richard
93 Regent's Park Road
NW1

David, Elizabeth Ltd
Bourne Street
SW1

See also Canterbury

Divertimenti
139 Fulham Road
SW3

and

68 Marylebone Lane
W1

Fenwicks of Brent Cross
Brent Cross Shopping Centre
NW4

Harrods
Knightsbridge
SW1

Mellor, David
4 Sloane Square
SW1

and

26 James Street
Covent Garden
WC2

Selfridges
Oxford Street
W1

See also Oxford

Lymington
Kitchen Matters
5 Angel Court
Lymington
Hampshire

Manchester
David Mellor
66 King Street
Manchester
M2 4NP

Newcastle
Fenwick Ltd
Northumberland Street
Newcastle 1

Norwich
Jarrold & Sons Ltd
London Street
Norwich

Quest Cookware & Gifts
1 All Saints Street
Norwich

Oxford
Selfridges (Oxford) Ltd
Westgate
Oxford

Penzance
Mounts Bay Trading Co.
8 Causeway Head
Penzance
Cornwall

Taunton
The Cook's Shop
2 Riverside Place
Taunton
Somerset

York
Fenwick Ltd
Coppergate Centre
Coppergate
York

Wales

Cardiff
David Morgan Ltd
The Hayes
Cardiff

Swansea
Treasure, Giftware
Bean Nash House
1 Caer Street
Swansea

Scotland

Aberdeen
Nova
24 Chapel Street
Aberdeen

Terracotta Ltd
Kitchenware
44 Willowbank Road
Aberdeen

Edinburgh
Jenners
Princes Street
S. St David Street
Edinburgh 2

Studio 1
Kitchen Shop
71 Morningside Road
Edinburgh 10

Inverness
The Highland Kitchen Shop
23 Baron Taylors Street
Inverness

INDEX

Note: bold type indicates the main reference.